Solomon Described Plants

Solomon Described Plants

A Botanical Guide to Plant Life in the Bible

"He [Solomon] spoke about plant life"
1 Kings 4:33

LYTTON JOHN MUSSELMAN

CASCADE *Books* • Eugene, Oregon

SOLOMON DESCRIBED PLANTS
A Botanical Guide to Plant Life in the Bible

Copyright © 2022 Lytton John Musselman. All rights reserved. Except for brief quotations in critical publications or reviews, no part of this book may be reproduced in any manner without prior written permission from the publisher. Write: Permissions, Wipf and Stock Publishers, 199 W. 8th Ave., Suite 3, Eugene, OR 97401.

Cascade Books
An Imprint of Wipf and Stock Publishers
199 W. 8th Ave., Suite 3
Eugene, OR 97401

www.wipfandstock.com

PAPERBACK ISBN: 978-1-7252-5576-0
HARDCOVER ISBN: 978-1-7252-5577-7
EBOOK ISBN: 978-1-7252-5578-4

Cataloguing-in-Publication data:

Names: Musselman, Lytton John, 1943– [author].

Title: Solomon described plants : a botanical guide to plant life in the Bible / Lytton John Musselman.

Description: Eugene, OR: Cascade Books, 2022 | Includes bibliographical references and index.

Identifiers: ISBN 978-1-7252-5576-0 (paperback) | ISBN 978-1-7252-5577-7 (hardcover) | ISBN 978-1-7252-5578-4 (ebook)

Subjects: LCSH: Plants in the Bible | Botany—Israel | Wild flowers—Israel | Plants | Plants, Edible | Plants, Medicinal

Classification: BS665 M87 2022 (paperback) | BS665 (ebook)

08/17/22

The following images are reproduced from Cambridge University Press, *A Dictionary of Bible Plants* with permission of the Licensor through PlClear: Aloeswood figure 6, Barley figures 4 and 5, Black cumin figure 2, Broom figure 1, Chicory figure 1, Coriander figure 3, Crown of thorns and thornbush figures 4 and 5, Dove's dung figure 3, Fig figures 2 and 5, Flax figure 1, Flower of the Field figure 1, Garlic figure 1, Gourd figure 1, Grape figure 2, Henna figure 3, Mandrake figure 2, Oak figure 5, Poplar figures 2 and 3, Thyine figure 1, and Wheat figure 2.

Soli Deo Gloria

Contents

Preface | ix

Acknowledgments | xi

Introduction | xiii

Plants of the Bible | 1

    Acacia | 3
    Algum | 8
    Almond | 9
    Almug | 13
    Aloeswood | 17
    Apple | 21
    Barley | 24
    Beans | 30
    Bitter Herbs | 35
    Black Cumin | 38
    Bramble | 41
    Broom | 44
    Calamus | 47
    Cane | 51
    Caper | 56
    Carob | 60
    Cattail | 63
    Cedar of Lebanon | 66
    Cinnamon and Cassia | 71
    Coriander | 76
    Cotton | 80
    Crown of Thorns | 83
    Cucumber | 88
    Cumin | 91
    Cypress | 93
    Date Palm | 97
    Dill | 102
    Dove's Dung | 104
    Ebony | 107
    Fig | 110
    Flax | 115
    Flower of the Field | 119
    Frankincense | 124
    Galbanum | 127
    Gall | 130
    Garlic | 135
    Gourd | 138
    Grape | 140
    Grass | 146
    Gum | 149

Henna | 151
Hyssop | 155
Juniper | 160
Ladanum | 163
Laurel | 169
Leeks | 172
Lentil | 175
Lilies | 178
Mallow | 185
Mandrake | 187
Mint | 189
Mustard | 191
Myrrh | 196
Myrtle | 202
Nettle | 205
Oak | 207
Olive | 211
Onion | 218
Papyrus | 220
Pine | 224

Pistachio | 229
Plane tree | 231
Pomegranate | 234
Poplars | 236
Reed | 242
Rue | 247
Saffron | 249
Spikenard | 252
Sycomore | 255
Tamarisk | 258
Tares | 262
Terebinth | 266
Thistle | 271
Thyine | 278
Tumbleweed | 281
Walnut | 284
Watermelon | 286
Wheat | 289
Willow | 299
Wormwood | 302

References Cited | 305

Bible Translations | 315

Subject Index | 317

Scripture Index | 325

Preface

This is a book describing Bible plants, the culmination of five decades of research on plants of the Bible. I love the Bible. I love plants. Put another way, I am a botanist writing about Bible plants, not a theologian writing about plants. The present work is a conflation of these two passions.

My goal in preparing this book is to provide a botanically accurate guide to all plants mentioned in the Old and New Testaments of the Bible. This has required original research with all the plants in their native habitats from Beirut to Borneo and from the Atlas Mountains to the Zagros Mountains. I have worked in all the countries of the Levant as well as parts of East Asia.

Some of the material presented in this book is from previous work, updated and with improved images. All the images were taken by me to provide the reader with impressions that would occur in vivo. As a graduate student I was told that if I publish anything there will be errors in it. I have found that to be true and have corrected several errors from previous work. I am, of course, culpable for any errors.

Acknowledgments

Any work that spans five decades and four continents will invariably involve a lot of contacts. I have received generous help and support from many people and cannot list— much less recall— them all. I can, however, note those institutions that supported me through their facilities, faculty, staff, and students as well as logistical support with travel and field accommodations. The Fulbright Program provided grants for the University of Khartoum, An Najah University, University of Jordan, and University of Brunei Darussalam. I was also a Visiting Professor at the American University of Beirut, Aleppo University, and the American University of Iraq-Sulaimani and a researcher at the Royal Society for the Conservation of Nature, Royal Botanic Garden-Edinburgh, and Nature Iraq. The breadth of support and encouragement from these was remarkable and was invaluable for my studies for which I am most grateful

I am especially thankful to the botany students who worked with me, among them Adl Eisa Awad, Kamal Ibrahim Mohamed, Hanni Abu Sbeih (deceased), Mohamed Al Zein, Khalid Al Arid, Peter Schafran, David Cutherell, Nabil Abdul Hassan, and Saman Abdul Rahman. I learned much from them and am pleased to see their continuing careers.

Omission of anyone or institution is cause for regret.

Financial support from several sources subvented Bible plant research including the Mary Payne Hogan Endowment at Old Dominion University, the Plant Research Fund at Old Dominion University (including the R. Daniel Peed fund), The National Science Foundation, and the cultural attache programs of the United States embassies in Damascus and Cairo.

My family has been consistently and patiently supportive without which this book would never have appeared. Thank you to my children and their spouses Jennifer (Mike), Rebecca (Jim), Sarah (Selim), and John (Virginia), as well as their children. There are more than subtle hints of plant interest in the grandchildren. But foremost I have to thank my wife of more than fifty years, Libby, who has given so much of her love, concern, wisdom, correction, and counsel. She is a superb cultivator and lover of plants and people and the love of my life.

Introduction

BOTANISTS IN THE BIBLE— IN THEIR FOOTSTEPS

There are two noted botanists in the Bible. The first is Jotham, who delivered a lecture on the slopes of Mount Gerizim (Judges 9) drawing on the well-known features of figs, grapes, olives, and thorns. The second is King Solomon, son of the warrior King David, who brought Israel to its zenith of military power. His accomplishments are exemplified in his wisdom, songs, construction of the temple and palaces, and writings.

Song of Solomon best displays the naturalist king's association with botany, irrespective of whether one thinks Solomon wrote it. There are references to twenty-three different plants or plant products in this short book of eight chapters. The *hapax legomena* (unique words in the Bible) include caper, henna, saffron, and walnut. The book of Isaiah mentions more plants (twenty-five), but it is eight times longer than Song of Solomon.

King David had a deep appreciation for nature. Several of his psalms are celebrations of the creation. Perhaps Solomon's love of nature, especially plants, came from David. The Qur'an also records David and Solomon's understanding of nature, but emphasizes animals, not plants.

Solomon may have drawn upon his knowledge of plants, especially trees, when designing and building the temple, considering the numerous timbers and plants used for construction and ornamentation in the edifice. He, however, did more than just use plants and cultivate gardens. "He described plant life, from the cedar of Lebanon to the hyssop that grows out of walls. He also taught about animals and birds, reptiles and fish" (1 Kings

4:33–34). In short, the Scriptures present Solomon as a student and teacher of natural history.¹²

Jotham and Solomon present two different aspects of plant science. Jotham used well-known crops like grapes and figs to present images of political realities. Solomon, on the other hand, apparently possessed a wide range of knowledge about plants, their ecology, and their uses. In addition to useful plants, Solomon appreciated plants in their native setting per the cedar and the hyssop. The Song of Solomon expresses a wide and appealing flora of symbolic, alluring plants, revealing something of Solomon's love for plant life.³ Both approaches are valid.

ETHNOBOTANY OF THE BIBLE

The balance between the Jothamic and Solomonic botany requires an ethnobotanical approach. Simply put, ethnobotany is the study of the *use* of plants—past, present, and future. This is a book dealing with the ethnobotany of the Bible. The most apparent use of Bible plants is for food, fiber, medicine, building. Less quotidian but significant uses are cultic and symbolic.

Uses of plants today are not always the same as in ancient times. Again, this is an ethnobotanical treatise, it is not a theological work dealing with the interpretation or hermeneutics of the Scriptures nor the philology of the original languages of Hebrew, Aramaic, and Greek. My goal is to improve the plant fluency for the serious reader of the Scriptures and to provide accurate botanical identification, especially for plants that have been variously translated. I also aim to show how each plant was used in Bible days, how it is used today, and to offer a survey of current research with references for further study. Ethnobotany has been a major concern of mine and I have tried to learn as much from the indigenous farmers and villagers as possible

---

1. Adapted with permission in large part from Musselman, *Solomonic Writings*.

2. At the beginning of the Enlightenment in England, Solomon was held up as an example for the newly developing investigative sciences. His pattern inspired Francis Bacon. In *New Atlantis*, Bacon describes a king named Salomon, who in the tradition of his biblical predecessor establishes a kind of research center called Salomon's [Solomon's] House. According to Bacon, "It is dedicated to the study of the works and creatures of God." The early establishment of the College of Physicians in London was known as "Solomon's House" and was an outgrowth of this idea. Musselman, *Solomonic Writings*, 26.

3. If Solomon wrote the book then this is obviously the case, but even if he did not it arguably reflects something of the impact that his love of plants left on the imaginations of the educated within Israel.

in the different countries where I have lived and studied. While there are numerous books on Bible-era foods, treatments of Bible plants often do not include them. Being a wannabe gourmand, I present foods that I have personally tried.

I want to answer the questions, what did it look like? Smell like? Taste like? Grow with? How is it used? How can I learn more about the plant?

To do this, I use both pictures and prose. Pictures give not only a general overview of the habit of the plant but also habitat information. I have taken all the pictures. The text of each chapter includes aspects of the plant not discernible from images, as well as information of ancient and current uses and features I find fascinating. I pay particular attention to criticism of verses that have been variously translated. Because of my work on plants of the Qur'an,[4] I include some information found in both the Qur'an and the Bible.

I have tried to avoid botanical jargon and fortunately am not familiar with theological jargon. But I do discuss some of the arguments regarding diversity of views of translations of plant names.[5]

PLAN OF THE BOOK

There is an entry for each plant mentioned in the Bible. These are arranged by American English common names. Because of a diversity of common names for the same species, any serious study of plants requires use of scientific names, these are included as footnotes. Further, my own field work, especially that involving autochthonous cultures' modern-day use of these plants, has been updated.

In an earlier work, I reviewed Bible plant literature extensively.[6] In this book I include references where the interested reader can obtain current information on the plant. These reviews usually include earlier work making an extensive bibliography superfluous but allowing the reader to find references of interest.

The reader will notice that the length of individual entries varies. This is because some major crops, like grains, figs, and grapes are well-known

4. Musselman, *Plants*.

5. Botanical nomenclature is an arcane though essential part of botanical research. Students—and many professional botanists—are often turned off by the rules and regulations of plant naming, a process that has proven invaluable in providing uniform and ready global communication of plant names. Accordingly, I include the scientific name for each plant but not the accoutrements that are often part of that process (authors of plant names, families, and more).

6. Musselman, *Dictionary*, 1–12.

and unequivocal in translation. In other entries, the determination of the plant was unclear, and research has added new knowledge about the plant. Those treatments are longer.

TEXTS, PRETEXTS, AND THE ROLE OF ETHNOBOTANY

Writing with any authority on plants of the Bible and the Qur'an requires a familiarity with both the flora and the texts. Ideally, the writer should have training in both theology, textual criticism, as well as first-hand knowledge of the plants of the region—a rare combination. The person meeting the criteria of being both a theologian as well as professional botanist is George Edward Post, who authored the first modern flora of the Middle East.[7] His impact on Bible plant knowledge by users in the United States through his entries in Bible dictionaries—still in print—has never been carefully considered. In fact, a critical view of the interplay of botany and texts has seldom been argued.

Ethnobotany draws upon laboratory and technology skills and social science research methods from anthropology, archaeology, history, and more. I write as a plant scientist who values the increasing input from the social sciences for ethnobotanical studies.

The analytical techniques available to plant scientists today are astounding and include genetic analysis using DNA and archaeobotany—a melding of botany and archaeology that draws heavily on plant structural analysis to identify seeds, pollen, phytoliths,[8] even from charcoal artifacts. Chemical studies of remains of plant materials in ancient vessels have been used to determine the plant or plants used. One of the most intriguing to me is the chemical analysis of dental plaque to identify the diets of ancients, even providing evidence that bananas were available in Bible lands thousands of years ago![9]

One example of solid biblical criticism is Trever,[10] who helpfully pointed out how professional botanists (e.g., Moldenke and Moldenke)[11]

---

7. Musselman, *George Post*. Post was also a dentist, physician, and archaeologist—a true polymath.

8. Phytoliths are silicon derivatives that are distinct for groups of plants. In other words, these virtually indestructible particles can provide the identity of the plant long after other plant parts have decayed.

9. Scott, *Exotic Foods*, 7.

10. Trever, *Flora of the Bible*.

11. Moldenke and Moldenke, *Plants of the Bible*.

misunderstood the literary style of the texts. However, while bemoaning this lack of appreciation of the impact of style, Trever cites an example of *Juniperus oxycedrus*, "shrubs growing among rocky crags of the desert wastes,"[12] apparently unaware that *J. oxycedrus* is not a desert plant. I believe the lesson to learn is that *both* botanical and literary approaches are needed, and few people are professionally trained in both. Once again, we need a dose of humility when dealing with sacred writings.

Bible plants have little, if any, doctrinal impact. But innate winsomeness can influence the way Bible readers consider the Holy Land. In an intriguing review, Zorgati has studied the scientific shift from classical Linnean botany to a more scientific approach, especially the application of archaeology.[13] In what Zorgati calls the Green Line, the relationship between the plants of Scandinavia and the Holy Land were linked.

He is on to something. By knowing the plants of the Bible and how we might use them, a living link with the past is established.

TRANSLATION OF PLANT NAMES—TOWARDS A SCIENCE OF BIBLE BOTANY

While there is a large corpus of literature on Bible plants (of varying botanical accuracy) there has been little attention paid to the methodology of Bible botany. Translation of plant names needs to convey to the reader the imagery intended in the original languages. This is an area of great interest, but covering the pertinent literature is not possible here. A helpful review of plants of the Bible from a theologian's viewpoint is that of Basson, who opines on the conceptual metaphor "people are plants."[14] A clear example is when Daniel interprets Nebuchadnezzar's dream about an enormous tree, the prophet tells the king "You are that tree!" (Daniel 4:22, NIV).

Another example of the use of plant imagery is from the great Lutheran theologian, Kierkegaard, who wrote several pieces on the lily-in-the-field as a lesson in being silent before God and the different ways a poet

---

12. Trever, *Flora of the Bible*. The misidentification is ironic since Trever considers Post's work conflating theology and botany as exemplary.

13. Zorgati, *The Green Line*, 331–32.

14. Basson, *People Are Plants*, 576–81.

and a theologian use the image.[15] This has apparently been a theme among theologians for some time, e.g., Spiers.[16]

LOST IN TRANSLATION

A Bible plant exposition with an incorrect identification can lead to a misunderstanding of the text. Here is a personal example of how wording can gave a wrong impression. Luke 6:1, "And it came to pass on the second sabbath after the first, that he went through the corn fields; and his disciples plucked the ears of corn, and did eat, rubbing them in their hands" (KJV). As a child growing up in southern Wisconsin and nurtured in the King James Version, I wondered how the disciples could rub off the hard kernels and eat them. The corn I knew had large ears with refractory kernels. Only later did I learn that the English word "corn" originally was used for wheat and barley, where it is indeed possible to pluck the ears and rub the grains loose. While my story does not technically involve a mistranslation, it is an example of how word use must have meaning to readers. It is a concern of theologians.

"Botanical terms in the Septuagint [the Greek translation of the Hebrew Scriptures] reveal a mass of uncertain and sometimes contradictory data, owing to the translators' inadequate and inaccurate understanding of plants."[17] This statement succinctly summarizes the problem facing Bible translators. Since many plant names are culturally freighted, the difficulty is capturing the meaning of the symbolism while maintaining botanical accuracy. Most translations were made in colonial times to aid the culture of the colonizer. In this postcolonial age, there remains that tension between

---

15. Kierkegaard, *Look at the Lily*.

16. Spiers, *Flower Teaching*, 638; Trever, *Flora of the Bible*; Basson, *People Are Plants*, 576–81; Kirkegaard, *Look at the Lily*; Spiers, *Flower Teaching*, 638. See also Steinmann, *Arboreal Literature*.

17. Naudé and Miller-Naudé, *Lexicography and Translation*, 1.

botanical accuracy and the clarity of the passage being explicated.[18,19] Prado points out the benefit of considering esoteric botanical knowledge for a better understanding of archaeobotanical findings.[20] Pairing of botanists and translators is essential, and it is my hope that the present work will encourage this working relationship.

Careful philological studies must be paired with botanical accuracy. One of many examples is Basal who reports a black-fruit cane[21], unknown to botanists.[22]

PLANTS INCLUDED AND EXCLUDED

Plant names in the Bible have been interpreted in diverse ways. For example, caper is various translated as "caperberry" (the fruit), "caper bush" and "caper tree" (the plants), as well as "desire." And balm in Genesis 43:11 is variously translated as "gum (of rock rose)," "balsam," "medicinal resin," "rosin," and "storax." There are several reasons for this. Perhaps the oldest and most influential is the attempt by students of the Midrash to give scientific names to plants that are described in the Old Testament in very general terms. The Bible refers to *qôts* and *dardar*, which English Bible translations have often rendered as "thorns" and "thistles." However, thorns and thistles are specific plants found in Europe but not in Bible lands. In fact, the biblical terms are much more general, not allowing us to determine whether the plant is a thorn, spine, or prickle. A striking instance of botanical overreach

---

18. Naudé and Miller-Naudé, *Translations as Complex*, 193. "By placing the taxonomy of flora on a strong ethnological and ethnobotanical basis, the alterity of the incipient (source) text can be retained while the translation is made accessible and intelligible for the reader by the usage of metatexts like footnotes. In this way, as much as possible of the complexity of the text is conveyed to the reader." They use myrtle as an illustration of how this would be treated in translations for readers who did not know this Mediterranean shrub. See also Naudé and Miller-Naudé, *Translations as Complex*; Kahn and Valijarvi, *Translation of Hebrew Flora*, and Miller-Naudé and Naudé, *Alerity in Translation* for examples of post-colonialism cereals unknown in Korea. Prado, *Esoteric Botanical Knowledge*.

19. Kim and Lee, *Bible Fruits*, 149–50 and *Agricultural Products*, 441 provide a very interesting discussion of the complexity of making meaning for readers of the Korean Bible translation relative to fruits and cereals unknown in Korea.

20. Prado, *Esoteric Botanical Knowledge*.

21. *Arundo festucoides* is now known as *Ampelodesmos mauritanicus*.

22. Basal, *Flora and Fauna in Isaiah*, 20.

is how some rabbis suggested that the sacrifice of Cain ("fruit of the ground" in Genesis 4:3, numerous translations) was flax![23]

This botanical malpractice extended to the New World. There was widespread application of Bible names to plants indigenous to North America coined by European settlers well acquainted with the Bible.[24,25] Specimens of this include the use of "cedar" for species of juniper and "rose of Sharon" for a hibiscus native to the Far East.[26] More cases in point could be noted of plants that were unknown in Bible lands but have now become part of Bible plant lore like crown-of-thorns, which is a common houseplant, native to Madagascar, not the Middle East.[27]

A category of plants I do not consider to be mentioned in the Bible are those with narcotic qualities and purported entheogenic[28] properties, plants that induce visionary experiences, most notably marijuana and the opium poppy. More than a few people think that they are mentioned in Scripture and for some the vision-inducing usage of these plants receives some legitimacy from a link with a spiritual book. I receive numerous inquiries about the inclusion of these two plants in the Bible, often being told that I am wrong when I object to their being ascribed to the ancient text. Unfortunately, the articles that argue for their presence can be written without botanical knowledge, making errors such as equating ergot fungus[29] with manna.[30]

For example, opium poppy has been used in the Middle East since ancient times, and there are numerous archeological finds in Egypt.[31] But I find no evidence at all that opium poppy is in holy writ. This conflicts with Duke, who argues that "gall" (see gall) is the opium poppy, "a flower

23. Shemesh, *Midrash Plant Names*.

24. The same conflation of regional plants with those mentioned in the Qur'an has also occurred. Musselman, *Plants*, 18.

25. The source of transposition of scriptural names to that of local plants is well summarized in Dafni and Böck, *Revisiting Plants*, 3. "The old translators of the Bible, e.g., King James Version (1611) and others . . . were not familiar with the original Hebrew, nor with the flora of the Holy Land. So, sometimes, they mentioned names from their local floras; this might also have been done deliberately to make plants more familiar to their own readers."

26. Several species of *Juniperus* are called cedars. Rose of Sharon is *Hibiscus syriacus*.

27. *Euphorbia millii*.

28. Entheogenic plants have chemical compounds that alter consciousness and are used for spiritual development.

29. *Claviceps purpurea*.

30. Nemu, *Entheogens*, 119.

31. Merlin, *Psychoactive*, 305–7.

thriving in the Holy Land."[32] Despite extensive field studies in the Levant, I have *never* seen the opium poppy in a natural setting, only rarely as an ornamental in a flower garden.

Similarly, there is no biblical evidence that marijuana is mentioned in the Bible, though I have observed acres of it growing in Lebanon. Surprisingly, Duke does not treat of marijuana in his tome on medicinal plants of the Bible.[33]

While there is no mention of marijuana in the Bible, its presence in neighboring countries has been validated, e.g., Egypt and Cyprus. Trade from central and eastern Asia in ancient times is well documented. This almost certainly brought cannabis to Bible lands, either as hemp fiber or marijuana. So, my exclusion of "weed" does not mean that it did not occur and was not used.

The interest in medical uses for Bible plants is astounding as measured by the number of citations in Google Scholar in December 2021. For example, there are 17,000 for pomegranate, 6,000 for myrrh, olive 17,000, fig has 10,000. Remarkably, the only plant mentioned in the Bible as being used for medicine is fig.[34] The prophet Isaiah recommended a poultice of fig for King Hezekiah (Isaiah 38:21).

IN BIBLE LORE BUT NOT IN THE BIBLE

Another category of plants has been associated with the Bible for hundreds of years yet cannot verifiably be found in the Scriptures. I am referring to apple, mustard, and aloe. Though there is little evidence that either apple or mustard are truly Bible plants, because of the lore surrounding them I have included descriptions of both. In the case of the plant translated as aloe, this is a mistranslation of a Malay word for eaglewood, which is mentioned in both the Old and New Testaments where it is aloe in several translations and eaglewood in others.[35] See treatment of aloeswood.

Other plants long connected with the Bible are lily, rose, mulberry, and sycomore. These are discussed under lily-of-the field, lily-of-the valley, poplar, and fig. Additionally, there are plants ascribed to the Bible such

---

32. Duke, *Medicinal Plants,* 320–25.

33. Duke, *Medicinal Plants.*

34. It could be argued that the wine and oil applied to wounds is an indirect example of vegetal derived medicine (Luke 10:34).

35. True aloe is *Aloe vera.*

as sorghum and millet that were grown in Bible lands only as late as the Roman era and therefore are not included.[36,37] There is little support from archeology and literature that any of the millets were significant food crops in Bible lands. Moldenke and Moldenke suggest that proso millet was grown, a choice largely based on the ancient history of this crop.[38] Millet along with sorghum[39] has also been posited as the grain used in Ezekiel's bread (Ezekiel 4:9).

Some of the plants mentioned in the Bible are supernal, images of plants or purported plant products that are not real. Among these would be the burning bush, Aaron's rod that budded, manna, and the gourd shading Jonah, which are obviously not ordinary plants—they are literary devices, not botanical wonders.[40]

This is a truncated review of the objectives and sources for the present work as well as a discussion of trends in biblical plant research which I have incorporated into the corpus of this book. Writing as a non-theologian I have tried to conflate the biblical and translation literature with documented botanical research. An ethnobotanical approach to understanding Bible plants and their uses, both practical and cultic, is my raison d'être. Especially interesting and promising current researches include molecular and analytical approaches to studying these plants which shows that this field of academic endeavor, often considered erudite and staid, is far from static.

---

36. Many of these are in Shemesh, *Midrash Plant Names*. His comments regarding the dissonance of plant names are helpful: "The midrash literature was composed at a later period than the biblical occurrences, so that there was a discrepancy between the cultural, material, and agricultural world of the Bible and that of the rabbinical period. Moreover, communities that lived in areas that were distant from the biblical story's place of occurrence were not familiar with the nature of the region and its natural components. Hence, the sages of the midrash saw reason to mediate between the biblical world and the physical and cultural world of later generations" (ibid., 166).

37. Millet is a name applied to several unrelated grains, including finger millet (*Eleusine coracana*), bulrush millet (*Pennisetum glaucum*, the only grain in this list grown on a large scale, chiefly in Africa), fonio millet (*Digitaria exilis*), adlay millet (*Coix lacryma-jobi*), proso millet (*Panicum miliaceum*), and no doubt more. Thus, using the term "millet" without the corresponding scientific name is imprecise.

38. Moldenke and Moldenke, *Plants of the Bible*,

39. *Sorghum vulgare*, an important grain in the semi-arid tropics.

40. Lefrak, Mikaela. "Is this biblical food the next foodie fad? This chef thinks so." *Washington Post*, August 7, 2018.

PLANTS OF THE BIBLE

ACACIA

Acacias are a large group of trees and shrubs found mainly in the arid and semiarid regions of Africa and also in Australia. They are often keystone species, that is, impacting local ecology in a manner disproportionate to their biomass. About five species of acacias grow in the Middle East and Sinai.

Leaves are small, an adaptation helping the plant conserve water. In times of water stress, the tree can drop its leaves. Flowers are white or yellow and borne in dense head-like clusters. Middle East acacias are armed with thorns and prickles, armament to prevent predation where food plants for insects and animals are limited.

Slow growing in desert conditions makes the wood hard and dense, therefore heavy. The heartwood of acacia is dark red-brown and attractive when polished. The deep color is due to deposits of metabolic wastes that act as preservatives, rendering the wood unpalatable to insects and resistant to water and fungi. Because acacia wood is especially durable, it is used in Sudan and other places in Sahelian Africa as a writing board. These qualities were essential in the construction of the tabernacle.

The tabernacle is the system of tents used by the Children of Israel in the wilderness. It provided a portable worship center with poles and stakes that could be set up almost anywhere. The only wood used in the tabernacle was acacia wood. Based on present distribution of acacias in the Sinai, the white-thorn acacia is a likely source of wood.

All structural features of the tabernacle—the ark of the covenant, the table of showbread and its poles, the brazen altar and its poles, the incense altar and its poles, and all the poles for the hanging of the curtains as well as the supports—were made of acacia. This wood is mentioned only in connection with the tabernacle (Exodus 37–38) and perhaps Noah's ark. Because of the weight of acacia wood, Homan suggests that the structural components of the tabernacle were not solid, but smaller pieces joined together. If solid wood were used, the structure could collapse under its own weight, and transport of the heavy pieces in the wilderness would have also been a problem.[1]

1. Homan, *Tabernacle*.

Acacia wood was commonly used in ancient Egypt[2] for a variety of applications, including boat building. I have seen acacia used to build boats in Khartoum, Sudan. It has been suggested that the shittim wood used in Noah's ark was from an acacia. The Arabic for some species is *shittah*.

Figure 1. Twisted acacia,[3] Wadi Feinan, Jordan. These trees are conspicuous in the desert because of their solitary growth and often slanted or flat tops. There is evidence that this wadi was the site of copper smelting and that acacia were used as fuel.

2. Gale et al., *Wood*, 334–71.
3. *Acacia tortilis*, now known as *Vachellia tortilis*.

Figure 2 Red acacia[4] near Worata, Ethiopia showing prominent thorns.

Figure 3. Stump of red acacia showing the dense red heartwood.

4. *Acacia seyal,* now known as *Vachellia seyal.*

Figure 4. A Sudanese man copying verses on to an acacia writing board.

Figure 5. White-thorn acacia[5] near Namutoni, Namibia.

5. *Acacia alba*, now known as *Faidherbia alba*.

Figure 6 Fruits. These are a valued food source for game as well as cattle. This species is widespread in Africa and reaches its northern limit in the Middle East.

ALGUM

The words untranslated algum and almug (see Almug) are the most mysterious woods in the scriptures. Most Bible versions leave the words untranslated (ASV, ESV, KJV, NASB, NIV). Sandalwood is used for both in the Darby translation. The NLT uses red sandalwood, also known as rosewood.

I am unaware anyone has suggested that almug and algum might represent two different trees. My reason for positing this is based on the context of the verses. The word is used only for the timber requested from Hiram King of Tyre. "Send me also cedar, pine, and algum logs from Lebanon, for I know that your men are skilled in cutting timber there. My men will work with yours to provide me with plenty of lumber, because the temple I build must be large and magnificent. I will give your servants, the woodsmen who cut the timber, twenty thousand cors of ground wheat, twenty thousand cors of barley, twenty thousand baths of wine, and twenty thousand baths of olive oil" (2 Chronicles 2:8–11 NIV). The verse suggests that the logs were to be cut from Mount Lebanon, underscored by noting the wages paid to "your servants, the woodsmen who cut the timber."

A putative candidate for algum is boxwood,[1] a well-known and widespread understory shrub or small tree used for hedges and topiary[2] in the north temperate region. The leaves are small, shiny, and evergreen.[3] The wood is hard and durable, with an attractive grain making it in demand for musical instruments, furniture, and artifacts.[4] Its importance in pharaonic Egypt has been well documented.[5,6]

In addition to its recorded use in Egypt, further support for algum as boxwood is found in Moorey,[7] who noted that Amanus, the mountain to the north of the Lebanon ridge in what is now modern-day Turkey, was

1. *Buxus sempervirens.*

2. Boxwood is the major subject in the journal appropriately entitled *Topiarus*, published by the European Boxwood and Topiary Society.

3. Braimbridge, *Boxwood the Plant.*

4. Braimbridge, *Boxwood in Roman Times.*

5. Gale et al., *Egyptian Wood,* 337–38.

6. Braimbridge, *Boxwood in Bible Times.*

7. Moorey, *Ancient Mesopotamia,* 350.

recorded in the Annals of Tiglath-Pileser II as "The Boxwood Mountain." Boxwood was present in the area, but never a dominant tree.[8]

Figure 1. Boxwood shrubs at the National Arboretum, Washington, DC.

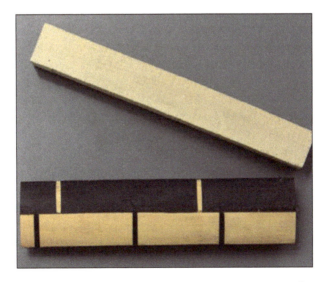

Figure 2 Boxwood (light), and inlay of boxwood and ebony.[9]

8. Rowton, *Mesopotamian Forests*, 271. "From the Lebanon, a cypress mountain, all the way up into the southern Amanus, the coastal mountains constituted the cypress and boxwood region. The utilitarian element is conspicuous. It can be seen in the emphasis on boxwood which was in great demand but nowhere a dominant tree, and it shows also in the designation of Lebanon as a cypress mountain, certainly never a dominant tree there."

9. My thanks to Professor Brad Embry for preparing these wood specimens.

ALMOND

The almond is the first fruit tree to flower in the lands of the Bible, and is a well-known symbol of resurrection. In fact, because it flowers as early as January, it is sometimes possible to see almond flowers on snow-covered branches. Almond[1] is a medium-sized tree with narrow, light-green leaves. Unlike the fig and olive, it does not live to a great age. The white or slightly pink, five-part flowers are up to 2 inches (5 centimeters) across and appear in the late winter before the leaves of the tree develop. Almonds are self-incompatible so fruit production is dependent on bees.[2] Almond growers often keep beehives near their orchards to ensure that flowers are pollinated. They have been cultivated for millennia[3,4] and are widely appreciated for their nutritive value.[5]

Within a month after flowering, the almond's distinctive hairy, green fruits begin to develop. These immature fruits have a pleasantly sour taste and are sold by street vendors as a popular snack in the Middle East. My children enjoyed them when attending a Palestinian grade school. In the middle of August, the leaves begin to fall, and the mature nuts are harvested. Almond is related to stone fruit trees such as peach, apricot, and cherry: the seed is enclosed in a bony covering derived from the fruit wall. But unlike those relatives, the fruit of the almond is unusual: the leathery outer covering splits at maturity, releasing the stone.

Almonds are mentioned six times in the Bible, only in the Old Testament. The first Bible reference is in Genesis 43:11, where Jacob orders his sons to take some of the "best products of the land" (KJV) as a gift to Pharaoh when they travel to Egypt to request grain. This early verse shows how valued these nuts were. The best-known almond reference is Aaron's rod that budded: "Moses spoke to the Israelites, and all their leaders gave him one branch each, twelve branches in all for their families; Aaron's branch was among them. Moses placed them before Yahweh in the Tent of the

1. *Prunus dulcis* also known as *Amygdalus communis*.
2. Company et al., *Almonds Botany*.
3. Gradziel et al., *Almond History*.
4. Delplancke et al., *History of Almond*.
5. Barreca et al., *Almond Nutrition*.

Testimony. On the following day Moses went to the Tent of the Testimony and there, already sprouting, was Aaron's branch, representing the House of Levi; buds had formed, flowers had bloomed and almonds had already ripened" (Numbers 17:8 NJB).

The most familiar component of the furniture of the biblical tabernacle is the lampstand, or menorah. The almond motif was part of the divine design for the lamp stand in the tabernacle. Moses was instructed to make the bowls of the lamp stand in the shape of the almond flower. The exquisite symmetry of the flower may be why almond is the model for the menorah. Almond buds and fruits were also to be present: "The first branch must carry three cups shaped like almond blossoms, each with its calyx and petals; the second branch, too, must carry three cups shaped like almond blossoms, each with its calyx and bud, and similarly for all six branches springing from the lamp-stand" (Exodus 25:33 NJB; cf. 37:19–20).

The reference to almonds in Ecclesiastes 12:5 is difficult to interpret: "When going uphill is an ordeal and you are frightened at every step you take—yet the almond tree is in flower and the grasshopper is weighed down and the caper-bush loses its tang; while you are on the way to your everlasting home and the mourners are assembling in the street" (NJB). The word translated "in flower" can mean two apparently contradictory things: the reference could be to masses of white flowers on the almond tree, which can be an allusion to the white hair of old age, or it could mean "to be despised."

Figure 1. Groves of flowering almond in northern Syria.

Figure 2. Almond is the earliest orchard tree to flower and is therefore a harbinger of spring.

Figure 3. Green almonds are a delicacy in the Middle East. Almonds of two different ages are visible on a Damascus vendor's cart, in March. Those on the left are younger. They are sold with a packet of salt in which the sour, green fruit is dipped.

ALMUG

Like algum, this is a mysterious tree or timber that has been subject to a variety of interpretations. (See Algum.) Some scholars think the same word is intended, the difference being in transposition of the Hebrew letters. But even if this were true, the origin of the two timbers, one from Ophir and the other from Lebanon, raises questions about the wood involved. The Lebanon source of algum remains debatable (see Algum), the Ophir shipment perhaps less so.

"Hiram's ships brought gold from Ophir; and from there they brought great cargoes of almugwood and precious stones. The king used the almugwood to make supports for the temple of the LORD and for the royal palace, and to make harps and lyres for the musicians. So much almugwood has never been imported or seen since that day"(1 Kings 10:11–12 NIV; cf. 2 Chronicles 9:10–11). From this we see that the origin of the shipment, but not necessarily the product, is Ophir (likely a place on the southern coast of the Arabian Peninsula). Ophir was the entrepôt for many different materials, including spices that came from the Far East. Second, the timber is linked with precious stones, clearly material from outside the Levant. Third, it is used not only in construction but also for musical instruments. Fourth, large quantities were imported. And it is important to see that this is included as an aside in the discussion of the Queen of Sheba, herself from outside the Middle East.

What, then, could this mysterious tree be? I suggest a candidate could be red sanders, also known as rosewood or red sandalwood among other names.[1] Three features of this tree in the biblical passage above give hints that fit red sanders. First, it was strong enough to be used in structural supports for the temple. Second, it came from Ophir, a well-known ancient commercial center for transshipment of materials from the Far East into the eastern Mediterranean.[2] Lastly, it was used for the crafting of musical instruments, a use of red sanders that continues to this day.[3]

1. *Pterocarpus santalinus.*
2. Anonymous, *Periplus*, 51.
3. Pullaiah and Divakara, *Red Sanders*, 19: "red sanders is in huge demand in the international market, especially in China and Japan, for the production of a special musical instrument, shamisen, with superior acoustic quality."

Red sanders is native to the Indian sub-continent with such a demand for its timber that it is now threatened. It is tall, reaching 50 feet (15 meters), reaching considerable girth (up to 5 feet/1.5 meters). The size of the tree yields beams that can be used in construction. The wood is considered one of the most beautiful in terms of color, which is deep red. In addition, the wood is hard, durable, and insect resistant. There is growing concern over the conservation status of this valuable tree.[4]

Red sanders is best known in India and Sri Lanka for producing a diversity of medicines. There is such demand that adulteration is frequent.[5]

An alternative to red sanders for almug is sandalwood.[6] Both were—and are—highly valued, red sanders for its beautiful color and grain, sandalwood for its scent as well as woodworking qualities. Favoring red sanders, however, is the production of large timbers useful in building. Sandalwood can become a medium-sized tree but is not traditionally used in construction. Sandalwood is native to the Indian subcontinent and is the source of one of the most valuable oils used in the perfume and incense trade. Either of these (among other timbers) could be the costly wood noted in the merchandise of Babylon in Revelation 18:12.

---

4. Arunkumar and Joshi, *Endangered Red Sanders*.

5. Pullaiah and Divakara, *Red Sanders*, 26–33. This is a helpful compilation of information on the uses of red sanders and includes numerous pictures of the wood and its products, both for artifacts and medicine.

6. *Santalum album*.

Figure 1. Red sanders in the Royal Botanical Garden, Peridenya, Sri Lanka.

Figure 2. Ayurvedic herbalist, Knuckles, Sri Lanka sectioning a piece of heartwood of red sanders to prepare a medicine. The red sawdust is on the floor.

Figure 3. Casket for jewelry carved from sandalwood.
Purchased in Thiruvananthapuram, India.

ALOESWOOD

One of the most distinctive and intriguing plants in the Bible has been frequently mis-translated. Aloeswood, also known as eaglewood and as agarwood (the name better used when speaking of the tree in reference to the Bible), has been called aloe, leading to confusion with the well-known aloe vera.[1] Aloe vera, a succulent perennial, is a frequent ingredient in cosmetics and herbal remedies and also grown as a garden plant. However, the aloe of the Bible is clearly a tree. True aloeswood comes from species of these trees, widespread in the rain forests of Southeast Asia. (The etymology of the term "aloe" is explained in López-Sampson and Page's discussion of history and use of aloeswood.)[2] The verses with aloeswood in Psalms, Proverbs, and Song of Solomon refer to fragrance, clearly indicating the plant is not aloe vera, which has an odorless sap.

The only uncertain translation is in Balaam's prophecy in Numbers 24:6. "As the valleys are they spread forth, as gardens by the river's side, as the trees of lign aloes which the LORD hath planted, and as cedar trees beside the waters" (ESV). It has been argued by some that the aloes here, translated as lign ("tree") aloes in the King James and aloes in the New International Version, could not be aloeswood for there is nothing striking about the appearance of the evergreen, tropical aloeswood tree. The Geneva Bible, the precursor to the King James Version, gives "tents" as an alternate reading of the Hebrew word *ăhālîm*, an interpretation used by some other writers. If very slightly emended, the Hebrew word can indeed mean tent. However, here the context seems to rule that out. The *ăhālîm* are clearly part of a list of different trees (alongside palm and cedar) and are said to have been "planted" by the Lord. Tents would make no sense in that context. Further support for the arboreal interpretation is found in Psalm 45:8 in which the same Hebrew root designates a substance with an indisputable role as incense. The Numbers verse is intriguing because it is the only reference to the trees of aloeswood (as opposed to the product produced from them). Further, in the Numbers passage it is linked with another well-known tree,

---

1. This is one of the few times the scientific name, *Aloe vera,* is the same as the common name, Aloe vera.

2. López-Sampson and Page, *History of Agarwood*, 108–10.

the cedar of Lebanon, which likewise did not grow in either Moab, where Balaam prophesied, nor in northern Mesopotamia, his purported birthplace. That this is botanical literary license is further evident by the fact that cedar of Lebanon does not typically grow as "trees beside the waters," but rather on mountain slopes. To object that aloeswood does not grow in the Middle East is to overlook the fact that it has been an important article of trade since ancient times and would be well known as an expensive incense and perfume.

Aloeswood is known in the incense trade by its Malay name *gaharu*. This has been highly valued since ancient times and was used both as an incense or a costly perfume.[3] Production of the scented wood is dependent upon a fungus that penetrates the tree either through natural lesions or by deliberate incisions into the bark. After several years, dark strands of infected tissue develop, this dense wood is the source of the fragrance. This hard, dark marbling contrasts with the light, almost spongy wood of the uninfected tree. So valuable is this product that tree rustling of infected trees supports a large clandestine industry even in protected forest preserves.

For example, in Borneo rustlers locate susceptible trees, then return at night to cut them down and process the *gaharu* (an activity I have observed). A single tree can fetch many thousands of dollars. Large infected trees are rare in the region even though they were once common components of the rainforest. Thankfully, a successful program of establishing plantations of aloeswood has been set up in several countries of Southeast Asia which hopefully will lessen destruction of native trees.

This product, used by ancients, is used in several religions. In addition to the Bible, the Hadith (sayings of the Prophet Muhammad) contains reference to aloeswood, both as a fumigant and as a medicine.[4]

The single reference in the New Testament involves the preparation of Jesus' body for burial (John 19:39), a practice consonant with the treatment of dead bodies in Roman times.[5]

---

3. López-Sampson and Page, *History of Agarwood*.
4. López-Sampson and Page, *History of Agarwood*, 111–12.
5. Caseau, *Incense and Fragrances*, 78–86.

Figure 1. Large *Aquilaria malaccensis* Sungai Liang, Brunei Darussalam. A strip of the bark has been removed by local people to make cordage, one of the non-incense uses of the tree.

Figure 2. Flower and buds.

Figure 3. Developing fruit.

Figure 4. Seeds. The white structure suggest that the seeds are distributed in the forest by ants.

Figure 5. Cross section of tree showing the dark strand of fungal infection, the source of the incense. The wood is light and of little use in construction.

Figure 6. Fragments of incense dense wood. The soft wood of the uninfected part of the tree decays in the forest, leaving these highly valued pieces for collection.

APPLE

The Garden of Eden and the apple are inextricably intertwined.[1] Yet apple is not mentioned in the first book of the Bible. The word does appear in several translations of Joel 1:12 and Proverbs 25:11. The apple is also mentioned in the Song of Solomon (2:3b, 5a; 7:8a; 8:5b). Or is it?

It is very unlikely that apple was a crop in Bible days.[2] There are two main reasons for this. The first is the climatic requirement. With origins in the mountains of Central Asia, the temperatures, especially the cold required for flowering, and the need for ample water proscribe the culture of apples.[3] Today apples are grown in the mountains of Lebanon and the Jebel Druze area of southeastern Syria. The second reason is the lack of convincing evidence for apple cultivation in Bible days, though apples assumed to be from Central Asia have been found at an archeological site in Kadesh Barnea in the Negev, a desert region not suitable for growing apples.[4]

It is worth mentioning here that the Hebrew word used in Genesis 3 for the fruit of the Tree of the Knowledge of Good and Evil is a general word for "fruit" (*perî*) and does not specify a particular species. So this is not an obscure word that we are unsure of its meaning. It is simply a general word that doesn't allow us to specify a species. And in this instance, the tree is not "ordinary" and species does not matter, save that it has edible fruit that looks good.

How did the apple become transported in Christian imagination into the Adam and Eve story? Foster traces the development of the apple in ancient times and how apple became grafted in a literary sense to the Garden of Eden.[5] The strength of this association is represented in the words of the Puritan poet John Milton, who wrote "It was from out the rind of one apple tasted that the knowledge of good and evil, as two twins cleaving

---

1. Recent taxonomic research findings require the scientific name *Malus × domestica*, synonymous with *Malus pumila*.
2. Brite, *Origins of Apple*, 168.
3. Juniper and Mabberley, *The Story of the Apple*.
4. Brite, *Origins of Apple*, 166.
5. Foster, *Symbolism of the Apple*.

together, leaped forth into the world."⁶ This is just one example from literature. The same is true in art representing Eve giving Adam the fruit, which is depicted as an apple in "Adam and Eve in Paradise" by Lucas Cranach the Elder (1509) and perhaps best known in "The Fall of Man" by Titian (c.1550). This perception of the role of the purported evil fruit is reflected in the Latin name given to the apple—*malus*, meaning evil. Schearing and Ziegler in their study of the theological and social impacts of the Garden of Eden also note that the apple is "a later suggested identity of the Garden's fruit."⁷ However, as explained above, the apple itself makes no clear appearances in the Bible.

The Hebrew *tappuach*, which appears in Song of Solomon 2:3 and 7:9 is sometimes translated as "apple." Could this Hebrew word actually refer to the apricot?⁸ Apricots can survive less rainfall and hotter temperatures than apples and they are fragrant, evidence that the so-called "apple" tree of the Bible could, in fact, be apricot.

Figure 1. Flowering apple tree in Jebel Druze region of Syria.

6. Milton, *Areopagitica*, 1644.
7. Schearing and Ziegler, *Enticed by Eden*, 9.
8. *Prunus armeniaca*.

Figure 2. Flowers of apple, Mancelona, Michigan.

Figure 3. Flowering apricot in Tel Tamar, Syria.

BARLEY

Two of the most important grain crops in the world—wheat and barley—evolved in the same region that gave rise to the holy scriptures of Islam, Judaism, and Christianity.[1] These grains are still cultivated on a large scale in the Middle East, so it is not surprising these writings refer to barley. While wheat remains the basis of life in much of Western Asia, barley is scarcely used today for human food in the region where it evolved.

But barley was a valued food in ancient times, as mentioned in Deuteronomy 8:7–9: "For the LORD your God is bringing you into a good land—a land with streams and pools of water, with springs flowing in the valleys and hills; a land with wheat and barley, vines and fig trees, pomegranates, olive oil and honey; a land where bread will not be scarce and you will lack nothing; a land where the rocks are iron and you can dig copper out of the hills" (NIV).

Both barley and wheat originated in the Fertile Crescent, that arc of remarkable agricultural resource that extends up the Euphrates River Valley, arches through extreme southcentral Turkey, and on its west lobe reaches down from Syria, through Lebanon in the Great Rift Valley separating Israel and Jordan. Agriculturalists now realize that the best way to conserve the genetic resources of these crops is in situ, where evolution of the crop can continue, while at the same time thousands of accessions of seeds are stored at national and international centers for breeding and crop improvement.

Barley's significance is also demonstrated by its being mentioned thirty-five times in nineteen books of the Old and New Testaments, yet it is the humbler grain, cited less than wheat, which is mentioned forty-six times, excluding references to bread. That barley was widespread and appreciated is plain in scriptural narrative; for example, the man from Baalshalishah brought barley bread and barley grain for Elisha (2 Kings 4:42), but Elisha ordered that it be provided as food for the people.

The phylogeny (evolutionary history) of barley is simpler than wheat. It involves a simple modification of the fruiting structure (spikelet), which prevents shattering, that is, fragmentation of the grain head at harvest, because

---

1. Zohary et al., *Domestication*, 51–66.

when grain shatters much of the crop falls to the ground and is lost.[2] The shattering wild barley of the Levant is now considered to be conspecific with modern-day cultivated barley.[3] In Bible days, most barley grown was hulled barley: the crop was harvested with the grains surrounded by the subtending bracts .(See Wheat on emmer wheat for preparation of hulled grains.)

Barley the Crop

Barley is planted about December in the Middle East, the exact date depending on the rains. The grain can be planted on soil without plowing, and for this reason it can be put in tiny plots in areas inaccessible to draft animals.[4] Further, barley can be grown in areas too dry for wheat. So, it is often seen in semiarid regions, such as the edge of the Wilderness of Judaea east of Bethlehem.

Barley matures as much as a month before the wheat, as noted in the Bible: "The flax and the barley were ruined, since the barley was in the ear, and the flax in bud, but the wheat and spelt were not destroyed, being late crops" (Exodus 9:31–32 NJB). In the Middle East, barley is mature by the end of April or beginning of May (corresponding with the biblical month Abib).

When ready for harvest, the fields can be a brilliant white, contrasting with the green of the durum wheat. Jesus was likely referring to barley in John 4:35 when he said, "Say not ye, 'There are yet four months, and then cometh harvest?' Behold, I say unto you, 'Lift up your eyes, and look on the fields; for they are white already to harvest'" (KJV). Among some recent translations, this allusion to barley fields is lost, and the fields are simply referred to as being ready for harvest. Jesus's original hearers, however, would have understood the allusion to barley when "white fields" were mentioned.

Barley Bread

In Bible times, barley was the main food of the poor and was also used for fodder (1 Kings 4:28). It was valued less than wheat: "Yahweh says this, 'By this time tomorrow a measure of finest flour will sell for one shekel, and two measures of barley for one shekel, at the gate of Samaria'" (2 Kings 7:1 NJB); and "Then I heard what sounded like a voice among the four living creatures,

---

2. Zohary et al., *Domestication*.
3. *Hordeum spontaneum*, wild barley; *Hordeum vulgare*, cultivated barley.
4. Though plowing may not be possible in these small plots, cattle were often allowed to press the seed grain into the soil.

saying, 'A quart of wheat for a day's wages, and three quarts of barley for a day's wages, and do not damage the oil and the wine!'" (Revelation 6:6 NIV).

For consumption, the Bible talks about barley being ground and baked into round cakes: "Gideon got there just as a man was telling his comrade a dream; he was saying, 'This was the dream I had: a cake made of barley bread came rolling into the camp of Midian; it came to a tent, struck against it and turned it upside down'" (Judges 7:13 NJB).

As noted in the dream, the usual shape of this humble bread was round. Barley has a low amount of gluten, about the same as emmer wheat, so barley bread does not rise much and is flat. About the time of the origins of Islam, rice became an increasingly important grain. Barley was widely grown, however, as a fodder crop. I have never eaten barley in any form with local people in the Middle East.

Yet barley is still an important crop. For example, in the vicinity of Bethlehem, small plots of barley are harvested by hand today, just as described in the book of Ruth, which has many references to barley. Boaz, a Bethlehem native, was a successful farmer, and barley was one of his important crops. Following the biblical injunction, Boaz left some uncut grain in his fields for the poor (Ruth 2:2, in accordance with Leviticus 23:22). Today, workers cut the grain, then tie it in bundles to dry. When dry, the barley is taken by donkey to the threshing floors, where it is threshed using modern equipment. If the ancient barley was a hulled barley, it could have been threshed with a threshing sledge pulled by an animal (Deuteronomy 25:4).

While the grain is less desirable for eating, the forage value of barley is much greater than that of wheat. In the United States, barley today is usually in the form of pearled barley (barley with most of the fruit and seed coat removed, which shortens cooking time), and is used in making soups, salads, and side dishes. Now considered a health food by many, barley is no longer just a food of the poor.

Beer

In the ancient Middle East beer was produced on a large scale due, in part, to the fact that grapes are more demanding in their cultivation.[5] The Hebrew word *šēkār* is usually translated "strong drink" and in almost all verses is paired with wine. But it is also translated as fermented drink, liquor, shekhar (a transliteration of the Hebrew), and beer. While dates can be fermented too, the overwhelming

---

5. Samuel, *Brewing and Baking*. This author did extensive studies of beer production in ancient Egypt. See too Homan, *Israelites Drink Beer*, who reviews beer production in Mesopotamia.

evidence of beer production in the region favors barley. Sprouted barley produces malt that breaks down the carbohydrates to produce alcohol.

To avoid being doctrinaire it is important to note that not only can beer be produced by dates, but distillation could be used. (Though there is debate over when distillation was first used in the Eastern Mediterranean.)[6]

Figure 1. Mature barley with scattered tares (green) near Latakia, Syria.

Figure 2. Winnowing barley near Adwa, Ethiopia.

6. Kockmann, *History of Distillation*.

Figure 3. Winnowing fork (left) and winnowing shovel.

Figure 4. Barley cake prepared with barley flour and water buffalo milk. Dodala, Ethiopia.

Figure 5. Barley bread from bazaar, Sulimani, Kurdish Iraq.

Figure 6. Barley beer in Ethiopia.

BEANS

The Bible places great emphasis on food, but little is said about vegetables and fruits. This does not imply those foods were less important than today, only that their description is not essential for the biblical narratives. Onion, garlic, melons, and lentils are mentioned in both the Qur'an and the Bible. This limited menu is puzzling since so many widely cultivated vegetables originated in the Middle East—foods that are now part of our daily diets.[1] Because it is not possible to know which of these beans are referred to, I am treating both broad beans and chickpeas here.

The best-known diet in the Bible is that of Daniel, who requested a vegetable and water meal regime (Daniel 1:12). How these vegetables were grown or harvested is not explained, though their cultivation must have been extensive. The sole vegetable garden mentioned in the Bible belonged to the evil King Ahab on property violently seized from Naboth the Jezreelite (1 Kings 21). Ahab wanted to take Naboth's vineyard and convert it into a vegetable garden, which is puzzling since the Jezreel Valley is very fertile and many sites could serve as a garden. Be that as it may, very likely one of the crops grown in such a garden was beans.

There are many different kinds of beans and it is not certain which bean is meant in 2 Samuel 17:28: "[They] brought bedding rugs, bowls and crockery; and wheat, barley, meal, roasted grain, beans, lentils" (NJB); and Ezekiel 4:9a (NJB): "Now take wheat, barley, beans, lentils, millet and spelt; put them all in the same pot and make them into bread for yourself." Based on archaeological data, lexigraphy, as well as current usage, it is likely that these are broad beans, also called fava beans,[2] and chickpea, also known as garbanzo beans.[3] These two well-known crops are discussed below.

---

1. Zohary et al., *Domestication*.
2. *Vicia faba*.
3. *Cicer arietinum*.

Broadbeans

Broad beans are a staple in the Nile Valley of today, where they are a traditional breakfast food. They are also widely cultivated throughout the Middle East and North Africa. Perhaps because the world now grows a number of different legumes—including peas, green beans, black-eyed peas, and soybeans—broad beans are not commonly sold in grocery stores, except those specializing in Middle East or Mediterranean foods.

After soaking dried beans to soften the hard seed coat, broad beans are boiled and eaten plain, added to stews, or mashed into a kind of gruel. Like other legumes, broad beans are highly nutritious and contain important proteins as well as fiber and carbohydrates. However, some people are allergic to broad beans, a genetic condition known as favism that can be serious and sometimes fatal.[4] Favism is most prevalent among people from the Middle East.

Sown in the late winter in Western Asia, broad beans mature in the spring or early summer. The plants are large and bush-like, with white flowers that yield large pods with broad seeds. The seeds, when young, green, and tender, are relished in the spring and are prepared like butter beans or green peas. Mature beans are brown and flat in shape and, when dried, like other legumes, can be stored for a long time. Two types of broad bean are grown in the Middle East: large seeded and small seeded. The small-seeded type is popular in the Maghreb and India, while the large-seeded broad bean is favored in Egypt and Sudan as well as in the Levant. It was no doubt from a store of dried beans that David was supplied (2 Samuel 17:27–28). Whether these and those referenced in Ezekiel are broad beans is unknown but not unlikely.

Chickpeas

Chickpeas are best known to North Americans as the garbanzo beans of salad bars or, with increasing popularity, as the basic ingredient of hummus. Chickpeas are an important part of the cropping system in many parts of the Middle East because the plants can mature on residual soil moisture after the rains have stopped. In some areas, two crops of chickpeas can be grown in a single year. Plants are short with small, grey-green leaves and inconspicuous flowers. The legumes ("pods") contain only one or two seeds. In Syria and Jordan, green, immature chickpeas are slightly roasted and sold as a delicacy by street vendors.

---

4. Luzzatto and Arese, *Favism*.

Both broad beans and chickpeas were important food crops in Western Asia thousands of years ago. The few references in the sacred texts do not accurately reflect the extent of their use. Like several other foods in the holy writings, they were essential nutrition for millions of people.

Figure 1. Flowering broad beans near Senana, Ethiopia.

Figure 2. Two varieties of broad beans. The large beans are favored in Egypt and The Sudan, the smaller are preferred in the Maghreb and India.

Figure 3. Chickpea in flower and fruit. International Center for Agricultural Research in the Dry Areas, Tel Hadya, Syria.

Figure 4. Pods of chickpeas. At this stage the seeds are immature and prepared like green peas.

Figure 5. Three different varieties of chickpeas. The smaller peas are the "desi" type and bear a fanciful resemblance to pigeon dung. The larger, more familiar, are the "kabuli" type. Samples courtesy of the International Center for Agricultural Research in the Dry Areas.

BITTER HERBS

As with many Bible names, it is not possible to say with certainty which plants are indicated by "bitter herbs." But the plant or plants represented by bitter herbs are still important in Judaism, based on the following verse regarding the Passover: "That same night they are to eat the meat roasted over the fire, along with bitter herbs, and bread made without yeast" (Exodus 12:8 NIV). From this verse, it is not clear whether bitter herbs were eaten raw (as tradition states) or cooked (not unlikely since both the meat and the bread were baked).

Many of the possible plants that could have provided these edible greens are bitter. Chicory,[1,2] native to the Middle East and common, has been suggested by several authors.[3,4] This plant is the source of commercial chicory (including radicchio) and inulin,[5] and because it is edible though bitter, it is a candidate for the bitter herbs associated with Passover.

Chicory is a widespread weed in the United States, gracing railroad rights-of-way and other open areas with its beautiful sky-blue flowers, likely it was introduced to North America as a crop.[6] In Egypt, where it is native, local people in the Delta region use this bitter plant as a vegetable and medicine.[7] This provides evidence for chicory as a bitter herb—or at least one of the herbs. It is now grown for the inulin, a widely used healthy fiber from the roots, a part of the plant that has been eaten for thousands of years.

There are many other plants that are known for their bitterness, including members of the mustard family and relatives of chicory, including wild lettuce. Lettuce is thought to have arisen in Egypt and is figured in

1. *Cichorium intybus.*

2. The taxonomy of the group has been studied by Kiers, *Chicory.* In a comprehensive review of the genus, she recognizes several species that some botanists lump all under *Cichorium intybus* as I do here.

3. Michael Zohary, *Plants*, 100. He describes *Cichorium pumilum.*

4. Koops, *Help for Translators*, 87. Koops uses the name *Cichorium pumilum.*

5. Puhlman and de Vos, *Back to Roots.* While the emphasis of this paper is on nutritional aspects of the plant, especially inulin, it also includes a fascinating history of chicory which the authors consider one of the oldest crops in cultivation.

6. Musselman and Schafran, *Edible*, 25–26.

7. Boulos, *Flora of Egypt*, 270–71.

pharaonic tombs and considered descended from the native prickly lettuce,[8] so called because of the armament on the leaves.[9] It was harvested from the wild by the ancients and is very bitter. Most of the bitterness has been bred out of modern lettuce.

Like other plants mentioned in a general way in the holy scriptures, care is needed when extracting meaning from a particular verse. In the case of this plant, clear identification is not essential for grasping its cultic use.

Figure 1. Chicory plants for sale in spring. Village store, Chouf, Mount Lebanon.

Figure 2. Wild chicory, Lake Bolu, Turkey.

8. *Lactuca serriola.*
9. de Vries, *Lettuce History.*

Figure 3. Prickly lettuce, Sur (Tyre), Lebanon.

BLACK CUMIN[1]

"Does he not finally plant his seeds—black cumin, cumin, wheat, barley, and emmer wheat—each in its proper way, and each in its proper place? The farmer knows just what to do, for God has given him understanding. A heavy sledge is never used to thresh black cumin; rather, it is beaten with a light stick" (Isaiah 28:25–28a NLT).

The Hebrew word *qetsach* used in this verse is translated "fitches" in the KJV, "caraway" in the NIV, and "dill" in the JND, but is most accurately translated as black cumin in the NLT. The word is found nowhere else in the Bible. There is little archaeological basis for translating *qetsach* as caraway (NIV). Caraway is not a Middle East plant, another indication of European translators' intercalation of plants known to them into the ancient texts. Dill is also a possibility and was known in ancient Egypt.[2] The same word is used for unrelated plants with similar architecture (pointed structures) in other scriptures (Ezekiel 4:9).

Black cumin is no relation to the well-known herb cumin.[3] In the Middle East, black cumin is planted in the winter and produces attractive flowers in the spring. This and related species are grown in the garden for their unusual flowers.

On Arab farms, I have observed farmers threshing the seeds of black cumin from the fruits by beating the dried plants with a stick in the manner recorded in Isaiah 28. The jet-black seeds are pungent, with a distinct flavor. Black cumin is most frequently used to flavor bread, cakes, or other baked goods. The spice is either incorporated into the dough or sprinkled on top during or after baking.

Black cumin is one of the most widely used spices in the Middle East and has been for thousands of years. Black cumin seeds were found in the tomb of Tutankhamun (1333–1324 BC). Medicinal uses of the seeds have received much attention recently, especially for tumor suppression.[4]

1. Also spelled cummin.
2. *Nigella sativa.*
3. *Cuminum cyminum.*
4. Ramadan, *Black Cumin Seeds.* Salehi et al., *Nigella Plants.* These are two of many contemporary compendia on the medicinal efficacy of black cumin seeds.

Like other spices in the Bible, black cumin is now popular and becoming increasingly available. Isaiah 28, however, deals more with the description of the farmer taking different actions at different stages of the crop's development, all with an eye toward the harvest. Pedagogically, this was no doubt clear to ancient hearers of the scripture, who would be familiar with the plants and the cultivating processes.

Figure 1. Black cumin in flower, Aleppo, Syria. The pointed beaks of the fruits are at the top of the developing fruits.

Figure 2. Threshing black cumin near Tubas (biblical Thebez), Palestinian Territories.

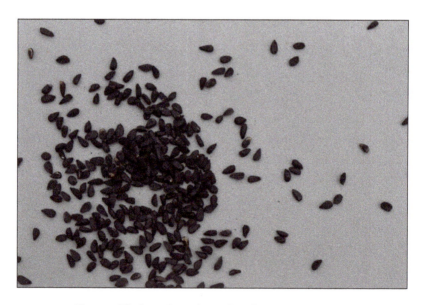

Figure 3. Black cumin seeds purchased in Amman, Jordan.

BRAMBLE

One of the first things an observer of nature would notice in the Middle East are the large number of armed plants: thorns, briers, and brambles. This armament (see Thistles) is necessary to avoid being eaten by the ubiquitous sheep and goats that roam the countryside. For this reason, the original audiences of Bible would get the point—literally.

"For every tree is known by its own fruit, for figs are not gathered from thorns, nor grapes vintaged from a bramble. The good man, out of the good treasure of his heart, brings forth good; and the wicked man out of the wicked, brings forth what is wicked: for out of the abundance of the heart his mouth speaks" (Luke 6:44–45 NIV).

Scripture does not often distinguish among thorns, briers, and brambles so this verse is helpful in differentiating thorns and brambles, although, again, we cannot be certain of the exact identity of any of these. Most likely the bramble plant we are considering in Luke 6:44–45 is the true bramble, a relative of the garden raspberry. Raspberries and blackberries are in the Rose family.

Bramble occurs in abundance in the Middle East. Flowers are white or purple and fragrant. The arching stems are armed with sharp, strong prickles. The fruit is edible but seldom collected, perhaps because bramble grows in dense, painful thickets.

A curse on Edom, recorded in Isaiah 34:13, also refers to brambles: "Thorns will overrun her citadels, nettles and brambles her strongholds. She will become a haunt for jackals, a home for owls" (NIV).

Figure 1. A wadi in Chios filled with impenetrable holy bramble[1] shrubs.

1. *Rubus ulmifolius* subsp. *sanctus*.

Figure 2. Although viciously armed, this bramble has attractive pink flowers and edible fruits.

BROOM

The bush that the depressed Elijah sat under is likely broom,[1] common near Beersheba, the locale where the prophet fled after being threatened by the evil Queen Jezebel: "So Jezebel sent this message to Elijah: 'May the gods strike me and even kill me if by this time tomorrow I have not killed you just as you killed them'" (1 Kings 19:2–4a NLT). Elijah was afraid and fled for his life. He went to Beersheba, a town in Judah, and he left his servant there. Then he went on alone into the wilderness, traveling all day. He sat down under a solitary broom tree and prayed that he might die. "I have had enough, Lord," he said. "Take my life, for I am no better than my ancestors who have already died."

Translated "juniper" in the KJV, broom, also called white broom because of its flowers, is a member of the bean family and is unrelated to juniper, a genus of gymnosperms that is infrequent in the desert.

White broom is one of the most common plants in deserts and other arid regions of the Middle East. The many tall (9 feet/3 meters), slim stems arising from the woody base bear small leaves for only a short time during the rainy season. Attractive masses of white flowers are borne at the end of the winter. With no leaves on the plant, the flowers are especially conspicuous. The entire plant is reported to be toxic to cattle.[2] Like many poisonous plants, broom is being studied as a source of medicines.[3]

The underground portions of the shrub are an excellent source of charcoal that produces an exceptionally hot flame. This use is mentioned in Psalm 120:3–4: "What will he do to you, and what more besides, O deceitful tongue? He will punish you with a warrior's sharp arrows, with burning coals of the broom tree" (NIV); and perhaps also referred to in Job 30:4: "They used to pick saltwort among the scrub, making their meals off roots of broom" (NJB). The Job passage is often translated as food from the broom

1. *Retama raetam*.
2. el Bahri et al., *Retama raetam*.
3. Léon-Gonzáles et al., *Genus Retama*. This is an authoritative monograph about the uses of the shrub reflecting the current interest in the pharmacology of the plant. Almost two hundred publications appeared since 2020 on the subject, according to a Google Scholar search (August 6, 2021).

tree, which is unlikely because of its toxicity. Rather, the meaning must lie in the use of the broom root as fuel. Broom wood was one of the chief fuels in copper smelter in the Early Iron Age (ca. 1200–800 BC).[4] Another study identified the wood used in copper smelting during five different eras and found that during the Persian era the majority of the charcoal samples recovered from the smelter were broom.[5] These two examples provide evidence of the value of broom as a fuel, especially since the biggest pieces are in the roots.

Because of its beauty and ability to survive under difficult conditions, *rotem*, as the white broom is called in Hebrew, is used as a girl's name in Israel.

Figure 1. Broom shrubs in the Wadi Arabah (Rift Valley) in Jordan in December when leaves are present.

---

4. Liss et al., *Broom Jordan,* 10.
5. Engel and Frey, *Copper Smelting,* 30.

Figure 2. Broom in flower, Amman, Jordan. The branches heavily laden with blossoms are often collected in the wild and sold in florist's shops for bouquets.

CALAMUS

Exodus 30:23, Song of Solomon 4:14, Isaiah 43:24, Jeremiah 6:2, and Ezekiel 27:19 are the only references to a fascinating plant, variously translated as "sweet cane," "calamus," "sweet myrtle," indicative of the confusion over which plant is intended. The Hebrew word, *qāneh*, is used to describe other, unrelated plants, with similar leaf shape. (See Cane).

The verses in the Prophets mentioned above clearly indicate the value of calamus and the fact that it was widely traded with nations in Asia. Two plants have been suggested for calamus. The first is a widespread plant of the Old World, calamus.[1] The second is lemon grass.[2]

Lemon grass is the common name applied to several different grasses producing a lemon flavor and smell. Much of the lemon flavoring in soft drinks is derived from this grass, not from lemons. In central Sudan, villagers use native lemon grass to thatch grass huts because the aromatic content of the grass repels insects. But I don't think lemon grass is the *qāneh* of the Bible. Rather, the plant in question is almost certainly calamus. It has an ancient history and was widely traded in ancient times,[3] strongly favoring this as the biblical calamus.

A plant of wet areas like margins of rivers and lakes, calamus is valued for the sweet fragrance of the rhizome from which various extracts are derived. In North America, the rhizome has been collected and candied, though the oil is recorded as being toxic. The sweet, lingering aroma is also suitable as a "carrier" in a perfume.

Song of Solomon 4:14 indicates that "calamus" was grown as a garden plant, which is understandable as the plant is easy to grow and is a common component of home gardens in many parts of Asia because of its use in Ayurvedic medicine. Sweet flag and its close relatives[4] have been used for

---

1. *Acorus calamus.*
2. *Cymbopogon citratus.*
3. Miller, *Spice*, 92–93.
4. *Acorus gramineus.* This species is widely used in China for medicines.

thousands of years and today are one of the most important plants in the Ayurvedic medical pharmacopeia still in much demand today.[5,6]

Figure 1. Calamus in flower. The tiny flowers are borne on a fleshy axis. Commercial field of calamus of an herbal medicine facility in Kathmandu, Nepal.

5. Cheng et al., "Acorus Taxonomy." This is a helpful overview of the ethnobotany, chemistry, and pharmacognosy of this group.
6. A search of papers dealing with the medical uses of sweet flag on Google Scholar gives over two thousand titles.

Figure 2. Field of calamus for commercial production of herbal medicine. Kathmandu, Nepal.

Figure 3. Ayurvedic medicine shop in Matale, Sri Lanka. The paper sac in the upper middle contains the dried rhizomes of calamus, the form in which it was merchandised in ancient times.

CANE

Plants associated with wetlands of biblical lands are interesting because of the limited wetlands in Western Asia. Some confusion exists over these plants' identity. Cane is an example.

The references to a measuring rod (e.g., Ezekiel 40:3, 5; 42:15, 19; 47:3; Zechariah 1:16; 2:21) are probably giant cane,[1] which is ubiquitous where any fresh water is found in the Middle East. The reference to "a reed like a measuring rod" (Revelation 11:1, NIV) supports support this use. Especially noticeable on hillsides because of its height, this plant marks a place where there is water even if not seen. Cane is not an aquatic plant but rather a species that must grow near water.

Giant cane can be tall, up to 6 meters (19 feet). It often towers above other surrounding vegetation. Stems are unbranched, straight, and woody, like bamboo, therefore suitable for constructing huts, walls, and fences. Cane was also used to make measuring instruments, a kind of meterstick (or yardstick) in ancient times, such as the man with the measuring reed in his hand in Ezekiel 40 and 42. Apparently, the man holds a giant cane because of its durability and utility. And in Revelation 11:1: "Then I was given a measuring stick, and I was told, 'Go and measure the Temple of God and the altar, and count the number of worshipers'" (NLT), referring to a reed like a rod, implying something stiff, likely cane.

In Exodus 30, in the recipe for the anointing oil, the same word is used. Clearly a different plant is intended here, a fragrant cane. The use of the same word for unrelated plants may be because the word describes the shape of the plant.

In the New Testament, the Greek word used for cane or reed is found in such passages as Matthew 27:48, where a sponge of vinegar was offered to Jesus on the cross: "And one of them quickly ran to get a sponge which he filled with vinegar and, putting it on a reed, gave it him to drink" (NJB). Another reference is Mark 15:19: "And they struck him on the head with a reed stick, spit on him, and dropped to their knees in mock worship" (NLT), where the reed was used for beating. In both cases, the plant that best fits the description is giant cane because of its length and strength.

1. *Arundo donax.*

This same word is translated "pen" in 3 John 13: "I have much to write to you, but I do not want to do so with pen and ink" (NIV). With a sharpened point, a piece of giant reed makes a writing instrument. I have purchased such pens made from cane in Damascus, where they are used for calligraphy. In some schools of Arab calligraphy, special emphasis is placed on pens made from giant cane. Cane is also used to make simple flutes and for basketry.

Figure 1. Cane is a true bamboo, or woody grass. It can form dense, impenetrable stands like this one near Wadi Rajib, Jordan.

CANE 53

Figure 2. Products made from cane are still used in construction in the Middle East and elsewhere. Here is a shop in Amchit, Lebanon specializing in cane. The partitions for walls can be seen in the center of the image. The furniture has woven cane bottoms. Cane is now being studied as a sustainable building material.[2]

2. Molari et al., *Cane Building*.

Figure 3. Calligraphy pens crafted from cane, in Damascus.

Figure 4. Simple flutes made from cane, from a shop in Damascus.

Figure 5. While botanizing near the village of Taybeah, Palestinian Territory I heard the shepherd boy playing his flute across the valley.

Figure 6. Cane (extreme left) and reed (projecting) in a mud and wattle building in Tel Amar, Syria.

CAPER

Caper[1] is widely used in Mediterranean cuisine. Is this plant and its products mentioned in the Bible? While the caper is common throughout the Mediterranean region, most Bible researchers consider it to be included in only one verse (but see hyssop).

Caper is a shrub with sharp prickles and large, attractive flowers that open at night, a feature of moth-pollinated flowers. It is unusual in losing its leaves during the rainy seasons and retaining them during the dry season.

So where might we find caper in the Bible? Ecclesiastes 12:5a—"when the almond tree blossoms and the grasshopper drags himself along and desire no longer is stirred. Then man goes to his eternal home and mourners go about the streets" (NIV). Most Bible plant literature (e.g., Zohary) equates "desire" with caper.[2] Thus, the word translated "desire" in the NIV is translated "caper" in other translations and is probably a metaphorical reference to a decline in sexual appetite and ability as a result of aging. There are many studies on the medical efficacy of this shrub and its uses,[3] and there is considerable evidence that caper is used as an aphrodisiac.[4]

The explanation for such use is easy to see. The showy flowers produce a true berry (botanically, a fleshy structure with many seeds) as a fruit. The fruit has a shape resembling human testes. According to the "doctrine of signatures," a plant part will affect the body part it resembles, a doctrine found in widely divergent cultures. Simply put, the fruit of the caper has a resemblance to human testes, ergo it is "signed" for medical use to that organ.

The largest producers are Morocco, Spain, Turkey, and Italy. The caper of commerce is the immature flower bud which has a pleasant pungency. I like the translation of the verse in the NJB: ". . . and the caper-bush loses its tang."

---

1. *Capparis spinosa*.

2. Koop, *Help for Translators*, 96–7; Moldenke and Moldenke, *Plants of the Bible*, 65–66; Zohary, *Plants*, 98; Hepper, *Bible Plants*, 50.

3. Nazar et al., *Caper Review*.

4. Moore, *Caper Products*.

Figure 1. Caper shrubs growing from a wall in Byblos, Lebanon. Because caper is so often found growing on walls it has been assumed by some that this is the plant often translated as hyssop that Solomon speaks of in 1 Kings 4:33.

Figure 2. Developing caper fruits. Yuppified restaurants are now using young fruits as a more interesting product than the usual flower buds. Mount Assos, Sulaimani Province, Kurdish Iraq.

Figure 3. Flowering caper near Al Bireh, Palestinian Territory. Floral buds, the source of pickled capers are present.

CAROB

The most frequent translation of word carob is husk or pod, an adequate description of the fruit of the carob tree.[1] This is the source of a chocolate substitute as well as locust bean gum, a common food additive.

Carob is widespread around the Mediterranean and its precise origins remain unknown, though perhaps in a hotter, drier climate than where it is typically found today. Because it is a valued crop, it may be more abundant now than in ancient times, as evidenced by the archeological record.

It is mentioned only once in the Bible, although there are suggestions that the seeds, which are remarkably uniform in size, were used in ancient times as a measure (gerah) as in Exodus 30:13 and Ezekiel 45:12.[2] In fact, our English word carat is derived from the Greek name of this tree (*keration*).

Carob can be a sizable tree, unique among its Mediterranean congeners in producing flowers directly from the stem. Most trees are unisexual and, understandably, there has been selection for the female trees in cultivation.

The fruits are long, flat pods containing numerous small seeds separated in the fruit by a gummy wall that is the source of much of the sugar and other carbohydrates. Traditionally, it has been used as fodder, as in the story of the prodigal son where carob was used to feed pigs. Ironically, what was once provender for swine is now a highly valued natural food.

---

1. *Ceratonia siliqua.*
2. Liphschitz, *Ancient or Newcomer.*

CAROB 61

Figure 1. Carob in flower. Carob flowers are small and unisexual. They often exhibit cauliflory, that is, flowers arising directly from the trunk as shown here in this staminate (male) tree on the campus of Stellenbosch University in Stellenbosch, South Africa.

Figure 2. Carob pods ("husks") and seeds. Because of the uniformity of seed size among trees, the seeds were used as measuring weights for gold and precious stones.

Figure 3. Carob tree with ripe fruits. Campus of the American University of Beirut, Beirut, Lebanon.

CATTAIL

Impressions of the Middle East do not conjure up images of cattails because they are associated with wetlands. Yet at least one species is widespread and may be mentioned in the Old Testament.

"Under the lotus plant he lies, hidden among the reeds" (Job 40:21 NIV) and "the lotuses conceal him in their shadow; the poplars by the stream surround him" (Job 40:22 NIV). The King James Version translates this verse as, "under the shady trees." This description of the behemoth includes its riverine habitat. It is unfortunate that NIV translators used "lotus plant" in this verse. Lotus is the common name applied to water lilies. But it is also the Latin name of a genus of legumes, *Lotus*. Species of this genus are not aquatic plants. So what is this mysterious plant linked with the likewise enigmatic behemoth?

Could the mystery plant be one of the other aquatic plants in the Middle East? In the context of Job 40, it should have the following features: form a stand dense enough to hide the behemoth ("under the lotus plant he lies"); grow in a stream that might flood ("when the river rages"); be part of a guild that includes poplars, possibly white poplar (v. 22); and be a plant compatible with vegetation found along the Jordan River (v. 23).

Of plants found under such conditions, the most likely is southern cattail.[1] It forms dense stands and has long, narrow leaves that would be within the circumscription of the Hebrew word for something slender. The thick heavy rhizomes can withstand flooding and it is a common plant in the Jordan Valley. It is also abundant in the Iraqi marshes where it has been used as a food for centuries.[2]

Whatever plant might be indicated, the obligate aquatic cattail is widespread in the eastern Mediterranean region and would be known to authors of the Bible texts.

---

1. *Typha domingensis*. I use the "common name" southern cattail under protest because it is misleading in implying it is plant of southern regions when in fact it is found throughout the world.

2. Pendergast, *Pollen Cakes*.

64   CATTAIL

Figure 1. Cattails[3] in a seep, Masah Oasis, Hajjar Mountains, northern Oman.

---

3. *Typha laxmanii*, tentative determination.

Figure 2. Mature fruits of cattail compacted together to form the well-known "cattail." The seeds are tiny and bear gossamer hairs for wind dispersal. A single fruit is near the top right hand of the image.

CEDAR OF LEBANON

Cedar of Lebanon is mentioned about seventy times in the Bible, only in the Old Testament, more than any other forest tree, which is intriguing considering it never grew within the traditional boundaries of Israel. But in a region of the world where forests were limited, cedar of Lebanon was widely famed for its beauty and its utility. Cedars are still the largest of any indigenous tree in the Middle East, though the populations on Mount Lebanon are a fraction of what they were in Bible days. These massive trees were likely the largest living things that generations of people saw during their lifetime.

These forest giants are an image of mighty rulers as in Ezekiel 31:3, where the King of Assyria is likened to a cedar: "Behold, Assyria was a cedar in Lebanon, with beautiful branches and forest shade, and of towering height, its top among the clouds" (ESV). Their strength was unequalled, so a measure of divine strength would be the breaking of the cedars, as in Psalm 29:5: "The voice of the LORD breaketh the cedars; yea, the LORD breaketh the cedars of Lebanon" (KJV).

Not only are the trees impressive, but their habitat is also one of great beauty. Because of its requirement for cool temperatures, cedar of Lebanon is restricted to higher elevations on the Lebanon ridge where it receives moisture as rain, fog, and snow from the westerly winds off the Mediterranean. The dark green trees and associated plants form a distinct plant community. This forest beauty and fastness is noted in several verses, e.g., Song of Solomon 5:15: "His legs are as pillars of marble, set upon sockets of fine gold: his countenance is as Lebanon, excellent as the cedars" (KJV).

The remoteness of the cedar forest is seen in a lament describing King Jehoiakim, who considered himself secure, like a bird nested in a high tree. This is pictured in the allusion to being discovered, even in a Lebanon forest. "O inhabitant of Lebanon, nested among the cedars" (Jeremiah 22:23 ESV).

Beautiful and living in a magnificent setting, the cedars were harvested mercilessly by every invader and used in imperial building projects. Cedars are slow growing with a solid heartwood and resistant to decay. They were the largest trees available in Western Asia. When Solomon wanted timber for his building projects, he contracted with Hiram, King of Tyre for the delivery of cedar logs for the construction of both the temple in Jerusalem (1 Kings 5) and his palace (the palace of the forest of Lebanon, 1 Kings 7:2).

Cedar of Lebanon was valued as a high-quality timber so its use reflected on the wealth and power of the monarch. In the days of King Solomon cedar is recorded as being as common as sycomore trees in the Shephalah (2 Chronicles 1:15, 1 Kings 10:27). This reference is obviously not to *growing* the cedars but to the *use* of the wood, as cedars would not thrive in the Shephalah.

While considering construction we should note Isaiah 14:8, where the prophet names trees as beneficiaries of Babylon's downfall. The king of Babylon had cut down trees on a massive scale and his fall means the cessation of such devastation: "Even the cypresses rejoice because of you, the cedars of Lebanon: 'Since you have lain down, the one who cuts does not go up against us'" (Isaiah 14:8). The trees are pictured rejoicing at not being felled.

Cedar is prescribed for several of the offerings, cleansing the leprous house (Leviticus 14), and the offering of the red heifer (Numbers 19). Recent evidence confirms the continued use of cedar oil into the Hellenistic age.[1] However, there is ample record of the extracts of both the juniper and related sources being used as well as cedar. This is utilized throughout much of its range as a folk medicine, including treatment of skin ailments. Both true cedar and species of juniper are confusingly referred to in English as "cedar." Meiggs provides a helpful review in the long-standing confusion between cedar and juniper.[2]

The legacy of cedar of Lebanon not only in the Bible but in other ancient documents and in folk botany is extensive. It is planted in suitable climates around the world. In its eponymous homeland, however, little of the original forest remains. Today, only about 3 percent of the original forest remains on Mount Lebanon with small populations in Cyprus and Syria and extensive forests in the Taurus Mountains of eastern Turkey.

---

1. Koh et al., *Cedar Oil*.
2. Meiggs, *Trees and Timber*, 410–16.

Figure 1. Lebanese geranium[3] forms dense stands in the Chouf Cedar Preserve on the northern end of the Lebanon ridge.

Figure 2. Cedar of Lebanon is adapted to the fog that forms as the prevailing westerly winds bring moisture in the form of fog at higher elevations. Chouf Cedar Preserve, Lebanon.

3. *Geranium libani.*

Figure 3. Developing cones. These take two years to mature when they then break apart and the winged seeds are distributed.

Figure 4. A large cedar in the *Horsh Arz el-Rab* (Forest of the Cedars of God) preserve near Bcchare, a site sacred to Maronite Christians.

Figure 5. Section cedar wood showing the darker heartwood and the lighter sapwood.

CINNAMON AND CASSIA

Like today, cinnamon was a valued commodity in Bible times. The present-day spice known as cinnamon is usually a mixture of two different species—cinnamon and cassia.[1] I find it difficult to distinguish between the aroma of the two, though cassia is less intense. The tastes are different. Cassia has a pungency that is lacking in cinnamon and the taste of the latter is more complex though less strong. Cassia (not to be confused with the unrelated genus of legumes) and cinnamon bark can be used as a spice as well as for oil, and oil can also be distilled from the leaves of each.

What is the difference between cassia and cinnamon? Miller suggests that cassia was more widely used in the ancient world because it had long been cultivated in China.[2] True cinnamon, on the other hand, was collected from the wild in the East Indies and was therefore more precious. Both were extensively traded over well-developed trade routes.

Both cassia and cinnamon are small trees but grown as shrubs for their bark and leaves. Stems are cut and the bark is stripped off and dried. Sri Lanka is the world's largest producer of high-quality cinnamon.

In addition to being a constituent of the anointing oil (Exodus 30:23), cinnamon was valued as a perfume, as in the harlot's bed in Proverbs 7, and the redolent garden of Song of Solomon 4:14. Likewise, cassia's fragrance is highlighted in Psalm 45:8: "All your robes are fragrant with myrrh and aloes and cassia; from palaces adorned with ivory . . ." (NIV).

As a valued object of trade cassia is mentioned among the merchandise sent to Tyre (Ezekiel 27:19), as is cinnamon in the traffic of Babylon (Revelation 18:13).

---

1. The cinnamon available in stores is often a mixture of two species. *Cinnamomum verum* is considered to be superior to *Cinnamomum cassia,* which is known as cassia. Cassia is sold at a much lower price than cinnamon.

2. Miller, *Spice Trade,* 42–47.

Figure 1. Flowering cinnamon in a plantation in southern Sri Lanka in March.

Figure 2. Flowering cinnamon, Sri Lanka.

Figure 3. The spice is derived from the bark of stems. Here a worker at the Cinnamon Research Station, Thihagoda, Sri Lanka.

Figure 4. Dried cassia leaves in herb market in Katmandu, Nepal. This includes leaves of *tamala*,[3] another kind of cinnamon.

3. *Cinnamomum tamala.*

Figure 5. Left, true cinnamon. Right cassia, sold as cinnamon. Notice the difference in the thickness of the bark. Cinnamon is thinner and stuffed with smaller bark pieces, while cassia is thicker and is not marketed stuffed with fragments of bark. Cassia is a frequent adulterant in ground cinnamon.

Figure 6. Bundles of cinnamon ready for shipping. Note how the center of the outer bark is packed with smaller pieces. Thihagoda, Sri Lanka.

CORIANDER

Manna and salsa? What do these two foods from different epochs and different cultures have in common? Coriander.[1] Salsa contains the leaves of coriander while manna resembles coriander. "The people of Israel called the bread manna. It was white like coriander seed and tasted like wafers made with honey" (Exodus 16:31). "The manna was like coriander seed and looked like resin" (Numbers 11:7 NIV).

Coriander is a widely grown annual crop in the Middle East and highly valued as a spice. The "seed"[2] is also used in the United States as a ground spice. Also familiar are the leaves of the coriander plant, which are known as cilantro. Cilantro is an ingredient of salsa and other Spanish and Mexican dishes. These two condiments, cilantro and coriander, are products of different subspecies.

Manna

The exact nature of manna is unknown. Perhaps the easiest explanation is that it was simply a divine provision, miraculously given. Or rather than being supernal, some Bible scholars have suggested it may have been the exudate of a desert plant.[3] But looking like "resin" does not support that view.

Also problematical is the relationship between the appearance of manna and the appearance of coriander seed. Coriander, at least the types now grown, have brown rather than white fruits. Thus, it is not certain if the Hebrew word *gad*, translated "coriander" in connection with manna, is coriander because the color ("white") and the appearance ("like resin") are at odds with at least the modern-day coriander. Recent work, however, shows that some varieties of coriander seeds can be white.[4]

---

1. *Coriandrum sativum.*
2. Botanically, it is technically a fruit.
3. Zohary, *Plants,* 142–43.
4. Arora et al., *Wild Coriander* 3, Figure 1.

I have purchased manna in a candy store in Sulaimani that uses the exudate of a steppe plant, saxaul.[5]

Figure 1. Coriander at the International Center for Agricultural Research in the Dry Areas, Tel Hadya, Syria.

5. *Haloxylon salicornicum*.

Figure 2. Coriander "seeds." Some varieties have slightly lighter, whitish color.

Figure 3. Saxaul, a widespread steppe plant in Western Asia. Because it is poor fodder, there are extensive stands. The white globs at the tip of the stems occur when an insect invades the plant. The saxaul exudate is a purported source of manna.

Figure 4. Manna candy. The label[6] reads: "Manna Manufacturing: after that the manna falls from the sky it is been collected by local villagers and it is brought to the cities to be sold to the factories that deal with sweet and in a result some manufacturing operations such as cleaning and washing and adding, it can be produced." The adding includes sugar, spices, and nuts. It reminded me of nougat candies.

6. Tofiq Halwachy, Mana [sic] Natural Sweets.

COTTON

The identity of the fabric used in the curtains of the palace in Susa in the story of Esther has long been debated. Some translations refer to them as cotton (ESV, RSV), others use white material, white cloth, or linen.[1] For example, the fabric in Esther 1:6 has been translated variously as cotton (ESV, RSV) or linen (KJV, ESV, DRA). Which plant is the source of the fabric?

Cotton is the most widely grown fiber crop in the world and one of the oldest non-food plants domesticated. Of the four or so species of *Gossypium* that are grown for fiber, the most widely grown in the United States and other north temperate regions is upland cotton.[2] In contrast, tree cotton is limited in its range, generally grown in small holdings in China, India, and Africa.[3] Unlike other cottons, it can become a rigorous shrub or small tree, hence the common name. It is likely—though not certain—that tree cotton was the species grown in the Near East.

This assumption is based on the record of King Sennacherib (704–681 BCE) boasting of having a tree in his garden that bore wool, almost certainly tree cotton, because it is better adapted to harsher environments than other species of cotton.[4] Tree cotton, though agronomically and in fiber quality less desirable than other species of the genus, is hardy and productive in arid regions and poor soils.[5] It is often grown in Africa where it can live for twenty years and attain a girth of 6 inches (15 centimeters).[6]

Some authors note that cotton was not grown in the Middle East until Roman times but was widely traded with Indian merchants.[7] Archeological studies in Bahrain strongly suggests that cotton was grown there. This is based on the discovery of woven cloth. This in and of itself does not document the local or regional growth of cotton. However, the presence of cotton

---

1. Koops, *Helps for Translators*, 146–48.
2. *Gossypium hirsutum*.
3. *Gossypium arboretum*.
4. Dalley, *Hanging gardens*, 163.
5. Blaise, *Tillage systems*.
6. Seignobos and Schwendiman, *Traditional Cotton*, 323.
7. Bouchard et al., *Bahrain Cotton*.

stems and equipment more likely used to spin cotton than flax gives strong evidence for the cultivation of cotton in Bahrain.[8]

The Esther story takes place in Susa in the province of Elam where the early use of cotton in the time of Esther has been documented.[9] Cotton was well known at the time of Ahasuerus (ca. 400 BC). Imported cotton was also available in Susa because of the location of the city along trade routes from India where cotton had been grown for centuries.[10,11] So, while it is uncertain if the source of the material for the drapes was from cultivated plants or plants imported from India, it is most likely cotton, rather than linen.[12]

Byssus

In the past few hundred years, terms translated as fine linen have sometimes been considered as references to true byssus, sea silk, woven from the fibers of a Mediterranean clam, the fan shell.[13] This is the rarest of fabrics with current production restricted to a few practitioners on the island of Sardinia. The cloth made from this mollusk has attracted a great deal of attention in the past quarter century.[14] It has a smaller diameter than flax, cotton, or wool, which makes it a very desirable, delicate textile. The name byssus has been used to suggest that this term in the Bible (e.g., Esther 8:15 [Heb. *bûts*]; Revelation 18:12, 16 [Gk. *byssos*]) refers to sea silk. Contrariwise, Maeder points out that the original use of byssus is for fine linen and that the term has inconsistently been misapplied to sea silk. There is, therefore, no indication that true sea silk is mentioned in the Bible.[15] The preparation of the ultra-fine yarn from hand-spinning flax "would be light smooth and semi-transparent."[16]

---

8. Bouchard et al., *Bahrain Cotton*.
9. Álvarez-Mon, *View from Elam*.
10. Kawami, *Textiles Iran*.
11. Quillien, *Cotton in Mesopotamia*.
12. Koop, *Flora in Ezra*, 237–39 reminds us that the curtains could reasonably be considered to be cotton, linen, or wool, as reflected in diverse translations.
13. *Pina nobilis*.
14. Maeder, *Byssus and Sea Silk*.
15. Maeder, *Byssus and Sea Silk*. Maeder gives helpful tables comparing the misuse of the term byssus in the Bible, comparing its use in English, French, German, and Latin translations, 8–13.
16. Cooke et al., *Spinning of Flax*, 22.

Figure 1. Field of cotton in northern Cameroon.

CROWN OF THORNS AND THORNBUSH

Thornbush is mentioned in the Bible and its identify is debatable. In the first botanical discourse in the Bible, by Jotham on Mount Gerazim (in modern day Nablus), five trees are mentioned: cedar of Lebanon, olive, fig, grape, and thornbush (sometimes translated as bramble) (Judges 9:7–15). The most likely plant for thornbush is Christ thorn[1] because it is a common component of the vegetation in that region where olives, figs, and grapes are also grown. Thus, it comports well both with the ecology of the region and with the literary image of a valueless tree.

It is a straggling shrub or small tree that thrives in areas of low rainfall. The plants are viciously armed with specialized stipules (modified leaf bases) in a curious way. One of the spines is straight, the other is curved. Often the only tree in the semi-desert, it is sought out for its shade.

Flowers are small, yellowish green, and can appear any time of year. The fruits are about the size of a small olive and are edible. In fact, some species of the genus are grown for their fruit, known in English as jujube. While considered a delicacy in the Middle East, I find the taste reminiscent of a mealy apple. Though thornbush is a possible candidate for the crown of thorns, thorny burnet (*Sarcopoterium spinosum*) is also likely a source of the crown of thorns, appealing as it is abundant on the hills around Jerusalem.

1. *Zizyphus spinichristi.*

Figure 1. Wadi Arabah north of Eilat, Jordan.

CROWN OF THORNS AND THORNBUSH 85

Figure 2. Wadi Arabah north of Eilat.

Figure 3. Ripening fruits Near Zababdeh, Palestinian Territory.

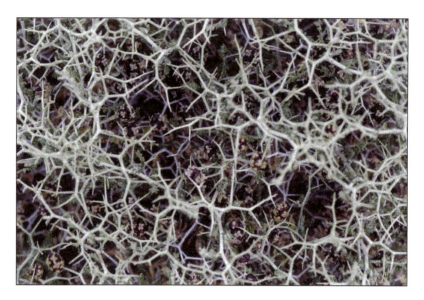

Figure 4. Thorny burnet, Island of Chios, Greece.

Figure 5. Hills above Jerusalem (barely visible in upper right) severely overgrazed leaving only the unpalatable thorny burnet. Al Bireh, Palestinian Territory.

Figure 6. Flowers of thorny burnet. The flowers are unisexual. The pink flowers at the top of the short flowering branch are female, the male flowers are below.

CUCUMBER

When reading the verses where cucumber is mentioned, the average English reader of course calls to mind the well-known vegetable[1] available in every grocery store—long, usually straight with a green skin, when young having prickles that are easily washed off. However, this is not the cucumber of the Bible. Instead, the Bible's cucumber is a very close relative of the common cantaloupe or musk melon.

There are two main varieties, one is yellow-green, long, curved, and usually hairy, known as snake cucumber.[2] The other is green and thicker and called chate melon, or less frequently snake melon.[3] It is used less frequently than the snake cucumber and considered a delicacy in parts of the Middle East. Both varieties have a characteristic fluting. And both are eaten fresh or made into pickles, similar to true cucumbers but with a milder flavor. They are also prepared as a cooked vegetable.

It is not clear which variety is the one mentioned in the Bible—the elongate, usually curved snake cucumber or the more "melon-like" chate melon. However, it is certain that chate melon was a common vegetable in Egypt, as documented by numerous images and models from that time.

Using linguistics, archaeology, and modern history, Paris and collaborators have traced the history of the chate melon from its cultivation in Egypt to introduction to Palestine along with the selection of longer, more slender cultivars in contrast to the thicker forms which the children of Israel longed for in Numbers 11:5.[4]

The inclusion of chate melon in the list of vegetables in Numbers 11 reflects the traditional diet at the time. The only other reference is in Isaiah 1:8: "Beautiful Jerusalem stands abandoned like a watchman's shelter in a vineyard, like a lean-to in a cucumber field after the harvest" (NLT). This reference indicates that chate melon was grown on a large scale and was a crop of value, as necessitating a watchman's shelter in the field.

1. True cucumber is *Cucumis sativus*.
2. *Cucumis melo* Flexuous Group.
3. *Cucumis melo* Chate Group. This species is one of the most morphologically variable of any crop, from Armenian "cucumbers" to muskmelon and honey dew melons.
4. Janick et al., *Cucurbits of Antiquity*, 1449.

CUCUMBER 89

Figure 1. Chate melon, the cucumber of the Bible, in Thale, Syria.
This form of the melon is favored when it is quite small.

Figure 2. Chate melons in a market in Suweida, Syria in June.

Figure 3. Snake cucumbers in a market. Courtesy Houssam Shaiban.

CUMIN

The spice cumin,[1] *derived* from the ground "seeds" (see below), is an essential component of East Asian as well as Mexican cuisine and for the same reason. Arab traders took the spice to India as well as Spain. From Spain, it traveled to the New World. But in the Bible it had cultic value as a tithe. "Woe to you, teachers of the law and Pharisees, you hypocrites! You give a tenth of your spices—mint, dill, and cumin.[2] But you have neglected the more important matters of the law—justice, mercy, and faithfulness. You should have practiced the latter, without neglecting the former" (Matthew 23:23 NIV).

Cumin is also mentioned in the Old Testament—unlike dill, mint, or rue. There is a great deal of similarity among the words used for cumin in Hebrew, Greek, and Arabic lending strong support to the identity of this popular herb. Cumin has been used for thousands of years in Egypt and surrounding countries.[3]

A relative of dill, cumin is an easily grown annual plant, grown for the seeds used to flavor bread and pastries.[4] It is mentioned three times in Isaiah 28: "When [the farmer] has leveled the surface, does he not sow caraway and scatter cumin? . . . Caraway is not threshed with a sledge, nor is the wheel of a cart rolled over cumin; caraway is beaten out with a rod, and cumin with a stick" (vv. 25, 27).

1. *Cuminum cyminum.*
2. Cumin is also spelled cummin.
3. Murray, *Egypt Condiments*, 644.
4. Technically the fruits, each "seed" is a mericarp, part of a fruit that splits rather than opening.

Figure 1. Field of cumin in the arid steppe at Khanessar, Syria.

Figure 2. Cumin harvest. The plants will be threshed for the seeds. Tel Hadya, Syria.

CYPRESS

Cypress[1] is a gymnosperm tree, widespread around the Mediterranean, where it has been used for construction of buildings, idols, and ships for millennia because of its durable wood and fine grain.[2] Very little remains of natural stands of cypress. As recently as the middle 1800s, when the Austrian botanist Kotschy visited Lebanon, he found large stands of native cypress[3] of which only vestiges now remain. It was also widely planted as an ornamental because of its attractive shape and evergreen condition. Since the time of the Romans the narrow form of the tree has been selected while it is generally assumed that the most frequent growth form had spreading branches.[4] This form can grow into a very large tree, comparable to cedar of Lebanon. Like its relative the juniper, cypress has a somewhat fleshy cone, globose in shape that opens to release the winged seeds.

Cypress was a prominent timber in the construction of Solomon's Temple (1 Kings 5 and 6), which was obtained by contract with Hiram, King of Tyre. It was used for paneling and flooring (1 Kings 6:15). The doors of Solomon's Temple were constructed of cypress, a frequent use of this wood in the ancient Near East.[5]

Some translations use pine rather than cypress (NIV) or fir (ASV). I believe the textual evidence favors cypress for several reasons. First, cedars and cypress were historically found in the same regions but at different altitudes. Cypress grows in a zone below that of the cedar, though natural stands of cypress are now very rare. This zonation is intimated in 2 Kings 19:23 and Isaiah 37:24, where both cypress and cedar are growing on Lebanon. Secondly, true fir,[6] is restricted in its Levantine distribution. The use of cypress wood in ancient shipbuilding is well documented and Ezekiel 27:5

---

1. *Cupressus sempervirens.*
2. Meiggs, *Trees and Timber,* 116–53.
3. Meiggs, *Trees and Timber.*
4. Farjon, *Monograph of Cupressaceae,* 223.
5. Meiggs, *Trees and Timber,* 70. Meiggs notes that translations for the wood used in the doors of the temple "have varied widely, but the choice lies between juniper and cypress and to me the evidence seems slightly to favor cypress."
6. *Abies cilicia.*

mentions it: "You were like a great ship built of the finest cypress from Senir. They took a cedar from Lebanon to make a mast for you" (NLT). Other uses included spears (Nahum 2:3). Finally, of prime interest to builders is the solid wood without knots such as characterize the two fire-dependent pines in the Middle East.

The beauty of cypress was appreciated by the ancients, as it is today. In a description of the beauty of Lebanon, cypress is mentioned (Isaiah 60:13). In Zechariah 11:2, cypress is one of a guild of glorious trees.

Figure 1. These very old trees are the widely branched variety. Slenfeh, Syria.

Figure 2. Branch of cypress showing the tiny, scale-like leaves.

Figure 3. This hillside grove of cypress shows the various branching patterns from the narrow (fastigate) to the more spreading. Efes, Turkey.

Figure 4. The brown areas are the male cones, the globose structures are female cones that contain the seeds. Most cypress trees have female cones that open in response to fire. Slenfeh, Syria.

DATE PALM

In structure, the date palm[1] is unique among all the trees in the Middle East. The single, tall, unbranched trunk with immense leaves, often over 6 feet (2 meters) long makes a striking figure, especially in a desert scene where other vegetation is sparse. Not only is the date palm beautiful, it is the basis of existence in desert regions and it provides construction material—with its leaves for thatching and its logs for construction—and shade.[2] In short, it is associated with desert civilization, one of the reasons it is the most frequently mentioned plant in the Qur'an.

The date palm is one of the oldest known fruit crops and has been cultivated for more than four millennia. As a result of such extensive artificial selection, it is not surprising that there is a great diversity in the species. In fact, an Iraqi Arab saying is that there are as many varieties of dates as there are days in the year.

Date palms are strictly unisexual, there are male and female trees. Since they are wind pollinated the grower usually has only one male tree among all the females. Because date palm sprouts from the base, the farmer knows the sex of the plantlet. In markets in the United Arab Emirates and Oman, farmers with male trees market the large branches of male flowers for sale. These are tied into the crown of the tree to ensure cross pollination and resultant fruit production.

The imagery of the date palm is used in both the Old and New Testaments in addition to describing geographical sites with groves of palm trees. Jericho is referred to as the "city of palm trees" (Deuteronomy 34:3; Judges 1:16; 3:13; 2 Chronicles 28:15), no doubt because of the oases there as well as the distinct climate—hot and dry. Elim (Exodus 15:27), one of the first stops after the children of Israel crossed the Red Sea, was characterized as having seventy palm trees. Such habitations were objects of beauty, Balaam likens Israel to a large palm grove (Numbers 24:6). The city of Tamar, modern day Palmyra in Syria, was captured and fortified by Solomon (1 Kings

---

1. *Phoenix dactylifera.*

2. Chao and Krueger, *Date Palm Review.* This is a succinct review of the ethnobotany of date palm.

9:17–19). The city's name is the Hebrew (and Arabic) word for date palm, *tāmār*, which suggests that it was a location associated with palm groves.[3]

Use of the massive leaves of the palm for thatching is implied in Leviticus 23:4 with the festival of Succoth and the building of booths, particularly interesting considering the long established used of palm thatch in the Middle East, even to the present time.

Remarkably little is recorded in the Bible about the eating of dates, though they have been used for millennia in a variety of ways.[4] Perhaps this is not surprising since many other sources of food were available, unlike in a desert situation. For example, date palm is not mentioned in the list of the six species of the land in Deuteronomy 8:8 though it is included in the list of food plants that perished in Joel 1:11–12, clearly indicating that it was an important food source. Ancient uses of the fruits include production of wine and a sweet syrup that certainly was used in Bible times.

The dates produced in ancient Judea were especially large and flavorful and considered extinct until the remarkable discovery of Judean date palm seeds two thousand years old that germinated, resuscitating a valuable strain of date palms.[5]

The palm is likened to a righteous person in the well-known verse in Psalm 92:12: "The righteous shall flourish like the palm tree: he shall grow like a cedar in Lebanon" (KJV). This imagery is not hard to envision—a tall straight tree, able to survive in the most trying circumstances, yet fruitful year after year. Song of Songs suggests this in 7:7 as well. Isaiah refers to the palm branch as the "honored man" (ESV) in Isaiah 9:14–15. Representing the honored or upright person may be why the palm is mentioned as the site where Deborah held court (Judges 4:5) and why the palm is such an important ornament in both the Temple of Solomon (1 Kings 6:29; 7:36; 2 Chronicles 28:15) and that of Ezekiel (Ezekiel 40:16; 41:18). (The reference in Hosea 1:13 has been variously translated and may not be the palm.)

The best-known passage of the date palm is Jesus' triumphal entry into Jerusalem when palm branches were cut and placed in his path (John 12:13). The people who did this would certainly have known of the imagery of the palm. This same imagery is found in the last biblical reference to this tree, in Revelation 7:9: "I looked again. I saw a huge crowd, too huge to count. Everyone was there—all nations and tribes, all races and languages.

---

3. I have not returned to Palmyra since its desecration by ISIS. Local merchants specialized in selling local dates to tourists.

4. Chao and Krueger, *Date Palm Review*, 1080–81.

5. Sallon et al., *Judean Date Palm*.

And they were standing, dressed in white robes and waving palm branches, standing before the Throne and the Lamb . . ." (NIV).

Figure 1. Masah Oasis, northern Hajjar Mountains, Oman.

Figure 2. Jimi Oasis, El Ein, United Arab Emirates.

Figure 3. Traditional house with mud and camel dung walls, beams of palm trunks, and ceilings of palm branches. El Ein, United Arab Emirates.

DATE PALM 101

Figure 4. Market in El Ein selling the male flowers of date palm. Since the tree is unisexual, growers keep very few male trees and supplement by buying male flowering branches, which they attach to the female branches on their trees.

DILL

Dill[1] is mentioned only in Matthew's Gospel: "Woe to you, teachers of the law and Pharisees, you hypocrites! You give a tenth of your spices—mint, dill, and cummin. But you have neglected the more important matters of the law—justice, mercy, and faithfulness. You should have practiced the latter, without neglecting the former" (Matthew 23:23 NIV).

While it is well known in the United States and Europe as a component of pickles, dill is widely grown throughout the world. Dill seed has also been reported from the tombs of Egyptian kings, documenting its long use in the Middle East. It is thought to have evolved in the region.

It is probably difficult for those of us living in the twenty-first century in the West with our ready access to herbs and spices from around world to understand how valuable these herbs were. Their reference in these verses on tithing by the Pharisees indicates their value.

Figure 1. Flowering dill.

1. *Anethum graveolens.*

Figure 2. Dill seed.

DOVE'S DUNG

"And there was a great famine in Samaria, as they besieged it, until a donkey's head was sold for eighty shekels of silver, and the fourth part of a kab of dove's dung for five shekels of silver" (2 Kings 6:25 ESV).

No vegetable item in the Bible has been subject to such wildly varying interpretations, ranging from the literal droppings of doves, the bulbs of the lily-like star of Bethlehem,[1] seeds of carob, to chickpea. Further confusing the identity of the "dove's dung" is its link with the donkey's head. There is at least one suggestion that the donkey's head could refer to a measure. This bizarre, and at first glance inedible, cuisine describes an extreme famine in Samaria.

The use of animal dung for food is, at the best, highly unlikely. In fact, pigeon droppings contain a plethora of diseases—and should the ghastly choice be necessary—would be the last of excreta to pick.

And the simple question can be raised that if there was an adequate amount of pigeon droppings, why not just eat the pigeons, a well-known food and a delicacy even now in parts of the Middle East. A more reasonable choice for dove's dung is star of Bethlehem, which produces numerous small bulblets reported to be edible after boiling. There are various references to the edibility of this plant, but an equal number to its toxicity. While it is common and well known by local people throughout the Middle East, I know of no report of it being eaten.

Another choice appears to me the most parsimonious and logical. Chickpea, also known as garbanzo bean, is an ancient and well-known crop in the Middle East. When dry, the beans resemble pigeon droppings, a similarity masked in recent years by unfamiliarity with an ancient strain of the crop. There are two main groups of chickpeas, the desi type and the kabuli type.[2] Of the two, the desi is the most ancient and is likely the type that was grown in Bible days. It bears a resemblance to dove's dung.

---

1. *Ornithogalum umbellatum.*
2. Singh and Saxena, *Chickpeas.*

Figure 1. Varieties of chickpeas. The large, pale seeds in the middle are the kabuli type, a more recently derived form, while the small black seeds above, and the row of brown seeds below are the desi type. Desi was the most widely planted variety in ancient times and bears a closer resemblance to pigeon dung than the kabuli chickpea.

Figure 2. Star of Bethlehem in my garden.

Figure 3. Each year the Star of Bethlehem produces bulblets from the parent bulb. These readily separate and are the reason the species soon becomes weedy in the garden or lawn. These are reported to be edible (I have not tried them). Other species in the genus are apparently toxic.

EBONY

"The men of Rhodes traded with you, and many coastlands were your customers; they paid you with ivory tusks and ebony" (Ezekiel 27:15 NIV). Ezekiel 27 is a wonderful look into trade and merchandise in the eastern Mediterranean. Among the material that arrived in Tyre were articles from the Far East, including ebony.

The wood in this verse has uniformly been translated as ebony,[1] a native of India and Sri Lanka, or a related species. An unrelated tree[2] is sometimes referred to as ebony, but it is African in origin and seldom grows to the size of true ebony.[3]

Ebony is one of the heaviest woods and is jet black, which makes it a prized source for furniture and artifacts. Ancient trade in ebony between the Far East and the Middle East is well documented.

---

1. *Diospyros ebenum.*
2. *Dalbergia melanoxylon.*
3. The link of ebony with ivory in the verse conjures up visions of African elephant tusks, but of course the ivory could have been harvested from Asian elephants.

Figure 1. Developing fruits on an ebony tree, Royal Botanic Garden, Peradeniya, Sri Lanka.

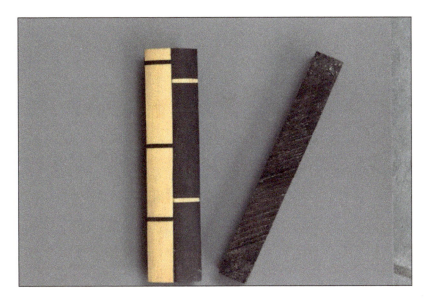

Figure 2. Right, sawn pen wood of ebony. Left, finished ebony with boxwood.[4]

4. Woodwork courtesy of Professor Brad Embry.

FIG

Figs are highly prized around the world for their sweet fruits. Because they are so easily bruised, figs are most frequently marketed as dried fruits. Due to their ubiquity and utility, they have a prominent role in the Qur'an and the Bible. In fact, one entire sura (chapter) of the Qur'an is called simply, The Fig.

There are references to the association of fig with testimony and judgement, a theme also present in the Bible. For example, the prophet Jeremiah told the people to submit to Nebuchadnezzar, who had conquered their land. If they did, they would be blessed; if not, disaster would come upon them. To make this point, two baskets of figs are set in front of the temple to signify two groups of Jews—good figs and bad figs. Those who, in compliance with the word of the Lord to Jeremiah, had submitted to the king of Babylon are regarded as good and would be planted in the land. On the other hand, those who refused to obey by coming under the authority of Nebuchadnezzar are symbolized by the bad figs (Jeremiah 24). Having one time ill-advisedly taken figs in my luggage from the Middle East to England I have a firsthand experience of what the bad figs were like.

Another example of judgement associated with figs is from the life of Jesus. The only thing Jesus cursed in his lifetime was a fig tree. "In the morning, as they went along, they saw the fig tree withered from the roots. Peter remembered and said to Jesus, 'Rabbi, look! The fig tree you cursed has withered!'" (Mark 11:20–21 NLT). Because the fig was so common in Jesus' day, his listeners would clearly understand the lesson.

In fact, the common fig,[1] is the most widely planted fruit tree in Bible lands.[2] The tree lives up to two hundred years so is often grown with olive trees, which are also long lived. It is a much-branched tree with branches arising low on the trunk. All parts of the tree contain a white, milky sap that

---

1. *Ficus carica*. The genus *Ficus* contains more than eight hundred species, including trees, shrubs, and vines

2. Goor, *History of Fig*. This is a helpful summary of the history of fig from pre-biblical days to the New Testament as well as information on the preparation of figs for eating and marketing.

can cause dermatitis in sensitive individuals. Leaves are about the size of a hand and have three main lobes and a hairy undersurface.

The fig is the last tree to produce leaves in the spring. While the leaves of the almonds and other deciduous trees are fully developed, the fig is just beginning to leaf-out. Jesus refers to this in Mark 13:28–31 as the beginning of summer, a verse often used to interpret Bible prophecies.

Why doesn't Jesus ask his disciples to look for the flowers of the fig? Because they are never seen by the casual observer. More than once when lecturing to Middle East audiences I have asked how many had seen flowers of figs. Most often the response is that figs don't have flowers! The flowers of the fig are so furtive that even the farmers who grow the figs have never seen them. That is because of the way that the reproductive organs of the fig are packaged.

The green unisexual flowers are contained in a specialized, fleshy structure known as a syconium or fig. The pollination process is one of the wonders of nature. A minute wasp, barely discernible with the naked eye, deposits her eggs in the flowers of the caprifig and turns these flowers into galls. A similar process takes place in the sycomore, another kind of fig tree. (See Sycomore.) The female wasps developing from the galls are fertilized by the males and leave through a small opening at the top of the fig. On her way out, the wasps must pass the male flowers and thus be dusted with pollen. They then carry pollen to the female flower to effect fertilization. Because the egg-depositing structures of the wasps are too short they cannot deposit eggs in the female flowers of the cultivated fig; while in the wild fig these are within reach and therefore are turned into galls yielding inedible fruits. Fruit production in the fig is thus totally dependent upon the wasp as a carrier of the pollen from the male figs.

Technically, the fruit is not a true fruit but rather a multiple fruit, as each of the tiny fig flowers develops into a separate fruit and these hundreds of tiny fruits together produce the fig. If the figs are not pollinated, they turn brown, and fall from the tree. These may be referred to in Isaiah 34: "All the stars of the heavens will be dissolved and the sky rolled up like a scroll; all the starry host will fall like withered leaves from the vine, like shriveled figs from the fig tree" (v. 4 NIV). Modern varieties of fig trees can produce delicious fruit independent of wasp pollination.[3]

The chief use of the fig is for its fruit, as we read in the divine commentary on trees in Judges 9, although it is also highly valued for its shade and, in the case of Hezekiah, was used medicinally as a poultice (2 Kings 20:7).

---

3. Falistocco, *History of the Fig.*

A fig tree may produce several crops in one year. There are many different varieties of figs—some with black fruits, some green, some red. Because the fig contains a high concentration of sugar, the fruits can be dried and stored for later use, a practice referred to several places in the Bible (e.g., 1 Samuel 25:18; 2 Samuel 16:1). The high sugar content may also explain the use of the fig as a poultice as in the case of Hezekiah's boil.

The fig is often associated with grapes and is one of the "five species" of the land (Deuteronomy 8:8). Blessing for Israel is often symbolized by the prosperity of the grape and the fig together (e.g., 1 Kings 4:25; Micah 4:4; Zechariah 3:1).

Luscious green, red, or yellow fruits belie the furtive nature of the sex lives of figs. The flowers are never exposed, and pollination takes place within a special chamber.

Figure 1. A young fig tree growing from the wall of the Omayyad Mosque in Damascus. The tiny seeds of the fig can lodge in the crevices of walls, especially limestone walls.

Figure 2. Fig in full flower.

Figure 3. Wasp larvae. After the insects leave, the fig will abort.

Figure 4. Ripening fruits of fig, Saladin Citadel, Al-Haffah Syria.

Figure 5. Flowering fig, Chami Razan, Kurdish Iraq.

FLAX

Flax was the most important plant fiber in Bible times. It is the source of linen. All cloth at that time was made either of linen or wool. Flax remains one of the most important fiber plants in the world because of the long, strong fibers found in the outer layers of the stem. These fibers are prepared by a kind of controlled decay called retting, which separates the fibers from the remaining stem tissues.

One of the common forms of retting in drier climates is allowing the cut stalks of flax to remain in the dew until the fiber containing layers separate from the stem. This is probably why Rahab had bundles of flax on her roof (Joshua 2:1). After retting, the fibers are cleaned and then bleached in the sun.

Flax is sown in the winter in the Middle East and flowers in the late spring. With sky-blue flowers that open only in the morning, it is one of the most beautiful of all crops and often grown as an ornamental.

Linen had several uses in Bible times. The most obvious was clothing. Other uses were for wicks (e.g., Matthew 12:2), as measuring lines, and cords. The man in Ezekiel 4 had a linen measuring line. High quality linen (based on fiber count in the yarn) exceeds the quality of modern-day linen fabric. This is all the more remarkable because these fine linens were made by hand spinning. These high-quality clothes were the desirable byssus of the ancient world. (See Cotton and Byssus.)[1]

But one use of flax not mentioned in the Bible is culinary. Apparently, the use of the plant from the earliest archeological finds indicate use as both an edible oil source as well as fiber.[2] This is striking as flax seeds, barley, and wheat are among the oldest known foods, well represented in archeological finds throughout the Middle East.[3] Oil, known as linseed oil, is expressed from the seeds of flax. There is now convincing evidence that the ancient Israelites grew flax for the seeds, which were cold pressed to produce oil.[4]

1. Cooke et al., *Spinning of Flax.*
2. Allaby et al., *History of Flax,* 59.
3. Zohary et al., *Domestication,* 101–6.
4. Kislev et al., *Flax Seed Production,* 583.

Despite the lack of any references in the Bible to flax being grown for food, there is a well-established tradition that the acceptable offering that Cain brought was, in fact, flax seed (Genesis 4:3).[5]

In many years of working in the Middle East I have never seen flax grown, which is remarkable given that it evolved in this region. It is unknown to local farmers, as indicated by an experience I had in the regional office of agriculture of the Palestinian National Authority in Tubas (ancient Thebez of the Bible), a region of intensive farming. One of my former students was the local officer and asked if I would please try to identify some seeds recovered by police from a man arrested and incarcerated on charges of growing marijuana. The seeds were flax! While a host of compounds, many excellent for health, are present in flax, no narcotics have been identified.[6] Hopefully, any attempts to re-introduce flax in the Tubas area will not result in legal action.

Unlike most other Bible plants, flax is no longer of any commercial importance in the Middle East and, ironically, linen garments sold in local shops must be imported from other regions.

Cotton was not widely plant until Roman times. See cotton.

Figure 1. Field of flax cultivated for seeds near Solay, Ethiopia.

5. Kislev et al., *Flax Seed Production*, 582.
6. Oomah, *Flaxseed*.

Figure 2. Field of flowering flax in North Dakota. This crop is being grown for linseed. The morphology of the crop is different from that grown for fiber, on which see Figure 27-1.

Figure 3. The sky blue flowers are one of the most beautiful of any crop.

Figure 4. Flax is grown for both fruit and fiber. Here are fruits (capsules) and seeds from flax near Adwa, Ethiopia.

Figure 5. Linen thread.

FLOWER OF THE FIELD

Spring in the Holy Lands comes early. By February, the hills filled with riotous masses of wildflowers. What a display! In fact, the hills above the Jordan Valley have one of the most diverse floras on our planet, with more different kinds of plants per unit area than most ecological systems on earth. One of the flowers that stands out here is the poppy[1] with its brilliant red corollas. This may be the plant referred to in the following verse. "All men are like grass, and all their glory is like the flowers of the field; the grass withers and the flowers fall . . ." writes the apostle Peter in 1 Peter 1:24. This fleeting bloom is probably the common poppy. Poppy may be confused with the common anemone.[2] However, the poppy is annual, while the anemone is perennial. (See Lily of the Field.)

Each poppy has a single flower, which rises from a prominent bud. Poppies are distinctive in having petals crinkled in the bud, like crepe paper. As they open, petals expand and smooth out. Within a day they fall off the plant, leaving the ground littered with the petals that soon dry and lose their color in the hot sun. Soon the distinct capsule develops with the abundant, small seeds dispensed through numerous pores. Within a week or so after flowering all that remains are the erect capsules, stirred by the hot dry air with no vestige of the once rich investiture of the flower.

In addition to its beauty, the corn poppy is edible. The seeds are used in baking and the petals are collected early in the morning to make a cough syrup.[3]

1. *Papaver rheoas.*
2. *Anemone coronaria.*
3. Grauso et al., *Corn Poppy,* 229.

Figure 1. Poppies in mid-day, some flowers have lost their petals leaving the developing fruits. Efes, biblical Ephesus, Turkey.

Figure 2. Poppies near Sulaimani, Iraq.

Figure 3. A field of opium poppies legally grown for medicine production. Near Yazilikaya, Eskisehir Province, Turkey.

Figure 4. Visiting the field with a group of botanists, I wanted to take a picture showing the exudation of the opium containing latex, so I successfully scratched the capsules and was almost immediately reprimanded by a Turkish colleague who pointed out that such fields were carefully monitored for activities like mine. Despite documented use of opium poppies in the Middle East there is no incontrovertible evidence that they are mentioned in the Bible.

Figure 5. Field of poppies near Paphos, Cyprus.

FLOWER OF THE FIELD 123

Figure 6. Dried poppy flowers (right middle) in the market in Damascus for compound medicines, especially for coughs. (The other containers are dried flowers for making medicines and herbal teas.)

FRANKINCENSE

Frankincense is prepared from the resin of several species of *Boswellia*, a genus of trees and shrubs native to the Arabian Peninsula and North Africa.[1] The incense is the gummy resin that can naturally ooze from the plant or mostly by cuts made to stimulate oozing. Milky at first, the resin dries into clear, hard drops, which are harvested about two months after coming from the plant.

The resin has several uses in addition to incense. It is used in small quantities to flavor certain candies and baked goods and also as a medicine to stop bleeding. Frankincense is a common commodity in Middle East markets, where incense is highly valued by local people. Despite the demand, all harvest is from native plants. Most of the frankincense is brought from the Arabian Peninsula and North Africa to market. Frankincense is one of the most highly valued natural products of the region and its harvest has reduced the population of trees and shrubs.

The formula given in Exodus 30 does not mention any quantities, only relative ratios of ingredients, all of which were to be in equal proportion. Salt was to be added, for reasons inexplicable.

The most famous appearance of frankincense in the Bible is, of course, its use as a gift from the magi, stargazing wise men from the East, given to the infant Messiah in recognition of his significant royal status (Matthew 2:11).

Modern day incense compounding still depends heavily upon frankincense. It remains as the most widely traded resin for incense, as in Bible days.

---

1. Thulin, *Boswellia monograph*, provides an up-to-date treatment of this fascinating genus.

Figure 1. Stand of frankincense in the Arabian desert in Dhofar, southern Oman. This is *Boswellia sacra*, usually considered the highest quality frankincense.[2]

Figure 2. The shrubby nature of the plant is evident here.

2. Thulin, *Boswellia Monograph*, 52–61.

Figure 3. Flowers of *Boswellia sacra*, southern Oman.

Figure 4. *Boswellia neglecta* with incision scars. This species of frankincense (there is no good English name) is a tree unlike most species, which are shrubby. Solomar, Ethiopia.

GALBANUM

"Then the LORD said to Moses, 'Take fragrant spices—gum resin, onycha and galbanum—and pure frankincense, all in equal amounts'" (Exodus 30:34 NIV).

The identity of the plant that provided this component of the holy incense remains mysterious, but most scholars consider it an extract of plants from the genus *Ferula* (also known as *Ferulago*),[1] a relative of dill, cumin, and other spices. These are attractive plants, tall with large masses of usually bright yellow flowers.[2] There are many species in Western Asia and around the Mediterranean, plants that have provided medicine and flavorings for millennia. The source of the resin is unusual—it is harvested from the cut roots. Asafoetida,[3] a well-known flavoring of Indian cuisine, for example, is produced chiefly in Iran and India.[4]

Galbanum was one of several ingredients in the holy incense, along with frankincense, stacte (see Myrrh), and "sweet spices" (about which little, if anything, is known). Even today, galbanum, chiefly from Iran, is used in the perfume industry.

---

1. Nair, *Minor Spices*, 186. Nair provides a list of *Ferula* species yielding galbanum.
2. Khojimatov, *Promising Ferula Species* has images of several species and their products.
3. Derived from *Ferula asafoetida*.
4. Khojimatov, *Promising Ferula Species*, 6.

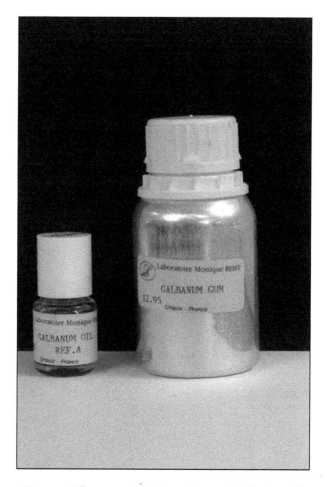

Figure 1. Galbanum used in the perfume trade in both an oil and gum preparation. Samples of galbanum gum and resin courtesy Laboratoire Monique Remy, Grasse, France.

Figure 2. Asafoetida in a garden in Cyprus.

GALL

Several plants indigenous to the Holy Land would fit the description of gall, meeting the requirement by tasting like bile. The references to gall in Job 20:16 and Lamentations 3:19 obviously refer to this bodily fluid (bile) and not a plant product. Candidates for gall from plants are opium poppy,[1] henbanes,[2] and poison hemlock.[3] Of these, the most likely is poison hemlock.

Found throughout most of Western Europe and Western Asia, poison hemlock is a perennial plant that grows to 9 feet (3 meters) tall and produces masses of small flowers on flattened heads in the spring. The stem of the plant has purple blotches, and the entire plant has a distinct odor something like carrots and parsley, relatives in the same family.[4] Poison hemlock is most common in wet areas such as the margins of ditches and irrigation canals. In the summer, the seeds (technically fruits) are produced and bear a dangerous resemblance to celery seed, cumin, and related spices in the same family. All parts of the plant contain the deadly toxin, coniine, which is a central nervous system poison, though it is especially concentrated in the seeds.

This toxicity is no doubt as noted in Jeremiah 23:15 and Amos 6:12b: "You have turned justice into poison" (ESV). Poisonings were frequent in the ancient world, and it is remarkable that none are mentioned in the Bible.

The weediness of poison hemlock is evidenced in Hosea 10:4. The KJV is one of the few to translate this verse as hemlock, perhaps because poison hemlock would have been familiar to those translators. And Socrates' suicide by drinking a decoction of poison hemlock would also be well known to them.

The incident with Socrates helps understand Matthew 27:34: "There they offered Jesus wine to drink, mixed with gall; but after tasting it, he refused to drink it" (NIV). The coniine in the plant destroys the central

1. *Papaver somniferum.* See Flower of the Field.
2. Species of the genus *Hyoscyamus.*
3. *Conium maculatum.*
4. Boskabadi et al., *Conium maculatum Poisoning* give an example of the toxic plant being confused with edible plants and also describe the symptoms.

nervous system and thus would be analgesic. The soldiers may also have wanted to speed the death of Jesus, though it is unclear why they would show compassion.

A second candidate is the opium poppy. Now widely grown in Western Asia, this poppy produces various opiates (morphine, codeine) and the poppy seeds used in cooking. There is little evidence for the widespread cultivation of opium poppy in the ancient Middle East. See Flower of the Field.

Figure 1. Poison hemlock in full flower near Antakya, Turkey. Despite the toxicity of the plant, the flowers are visited by numerous insects.

Figure 2. This stand near the walls of ruins in Baalbeck, Lebanon shows the weedy habitat of the plant.

Figure 3. Purple splotches on the stem and swollen leaf bases are distinguishing characters of poison hemlock.

Figure 4. The white flowers, borne in large masses, can be mistaken for the widespread and common weed, Queen Anne's lace.[5]

---

5. *Daucus carota*.

Figure 5. Fern-like leaf of poison hemlock.

GARLIC

Both the Bible and the Qur'an refer to garlic[1] in the same incident—when people complained to Moses about food (Numbers 11:5; Sura 2:61) and requested the cuisine they had enjoyed in Egypt, including garlic. This food certainly made an impression on them, as they were willing to consider a return to slavery so they could enjoy the good eats of Egypt. Likewise, any present-day visitor to Egypt would be impressed with the pervasive use of garlic in so many dishes characteristic of that country. It would not take many meals to know that garlic is still one of the most widely used flavorings in food in Egypt. Garlic can't be grown from seed and must be set out as bulbs.

Garlic is linked with onion, both in these scriptures and in grocery stores, but there are significant differences in their biology. First, garlic is sterile and must be planted from bulbs. Also, the structure of the bulb is much different in onion and garlic. The onion bulb consists of overlapping scale leaves while the garlic bulb is formed from the thickened leaf bases that develop within a common covering. There is considerable evidence that garlic was widespread in the ancient Middle East.[2]

The Hebrew word *shûmîm* (garlic) is an example of a hapex legomenon, a word mentioned only one time (Numbers 11:5). This is striking as there is no doubt as to the extent of use of garlic at the time this verse was written. But few foods are mentioned in the Bible, garlic being one example. Further authentication is the ubiquitous use of garlic in foods of the entire Mediterranean region.

---

1. *Allium sativum.*
2. Sarpaki, *Archaeology of Garlic,* 2–7.

Figure 1. A field of garlic in the early spring at Wadi Jhannem, northern Lebanon. The garlic is intercropped with arugula.[3]

---

3. *Eruca sativa.*

Figure 2. Garlic drying in a window in Hamah, Syria in early summer.

GOURD

The gourd, more accurately termed the colycinth,[1] is a common herbaceous vine found in dry areas. Like its close relative the watermelon, which it resembles in many ways, the colycinth creeps along the ground and has dissected leaves. The fruit is about the size of an orange with a yellowish rind, greenish pulp, and light brown seeds. Fruits are attractive, deceptively so. Unlike the watermelon, it is not edible. Foolishly, I tasted the pulp of the fruit and had a numb tongue for several hours. The taste of the flesh is extremely bitter but is readily available from Arab herbalists as a medicine.

In 2 Kings 4:38–39 the sons of the prophets had to prepare a meal for a large group and apparently at short notice. Without the necessary food in the larder, one of Elisha's disciples went out into the field to get some eats. As he was collecting various edible plants, he happened upon the colycinth ("gourd"). The result was a memorable dinner party where the guests thought they were being poisoned.

To be avoided as food, gourd is however an attractive plant, with a symmetry and beauty that has established it in various art forms. Gourds were used ornamentally in Solomon's temple (1 Kings 6:18a). I have also seen them used ornamentally in several of the famous Byzantine mosaics in Jordan.

It is not clear to me why a gourd would be the image used in the story of Jonah (Jonah 4). It is not an especially rapidly growing plant nor are the leaves exceptionally large.

---

1. *Citrullus colycinthus.*

Figure 1. Colycinth seeds in market in Kano, northern Nigeria. The ground seeds are used to make *egusi*, the traditional sauce served with pounded yam.

Figure 2. A ripe colocynth gourd, Aqaba Bird Sanctuary, Jordan.

GRAPE

The wine grape[1] is the most widely cultivated and economically important fruit crop in the world and has been the subject of intense study for millennia. Grape is the most frequently mentioned plant in the Bible.

No plant is more intimately associated with Christianity than the grape. In fact, in John 15:1 Jesus calls himself the true vine, an echo of the song of the vineyard in Isaiah 5. The imagery and lore of the grape is therefore well known, as is the chief product of the vine, wine. Wine was an essential part of the diet in ancient times. There are almost 250 references to wine, second only to bread with 350 references. What concerns us here is the plant and its features rather than its products.

The wine grape has multiple origins, one in the Near East and the other in the western Mediterranean area.[2] Unlike its wild progenitors, the cultivated variety usually produces bisexual flowers, which means that it can be self-fertile, though most propagation is by cuttings.[3] It is a woody vine that must be pruned in order to be productive.

Pruning is done in the late winter or early spring before the grape flowers, as suggested in Song of Solomon 2:12: "For behold, the winter is past, The rain is over and gone. The flowers have already appeared in the land; The time has arrived for pruning the vines, And the voice of the turtledove has been heard in our land" (NASB; most translations have "a time of singing" rather than "pruning"). In any event, pruning must be done early. That is why Isaiah 18:5 states: "For, before the harvest, when the blossom is gone and the flower becomes a ripening grape, he will cut off the shoots with pruning knives, and cut down and take away the spreading branches" (NIV). Pruning at this time would cause damage to the vines. The best known reference to pruning is in John 15, where Jesus speaks of the necessity of pruning if fruit is to be borne.

There are two forms of grape cultivation. The first, which is most common in areas of low rainfall, allows the vines to creep along the ground. This method does not require the effort and materials necessary if they are

1. *Vitis vinifera.*
2. Zohary et al., *Domestication,* 121–26.
3. Zohary et al., *Domestication.*

trellised. This is the way grapes are grown in poorer areas where resources for trellising are limited. On the other hand, yield is lower than when trellised. It is not clear if trellises were used in Bible days. A verse like Genesis 49:22—"Joseph is a fruitful bough, even a fruitful bough by a well; whose branches run over the wall" (KJV)—suggests a vine on the ground that can climb over a rock wall, a common scene in many parts of Western Asia.

The greenish, very fragrant flowers are produced in the spring, yielding the well-known fruit, technically a berry, in the late summer or autumn. Grape leaves are important in some Middle Eastern dishes, but there is no mention of their use in the Bible. The flowers, mature and immature fruits, vines, and wood are all mentioned in the Scriptures.

Because the cultivated grape can interbreed with less desirable varieties or even feral plants, an inferior crop may result, as suggested in Isaiah 5:2: "He dug it up and cleared it of stones and planted it with the choicest vines. He built a watchtower in it and cut out a winepress as well. Then he looked for a crop of good grapes, but it yielded only bad fruit" (NIV).

It seems likely that both green and red varieties of grape have been grown since the earliest times, but there is no explicit reference to green grapes in the Bible (not to be confused with unripe grapes, which are green regardless of the variety). A well-known inference to red grapes is Revelation 14:20 (cf. Isaiah 63:1–3).

The ripe fruit, which is rich in sugars, can be eaten fresh, as recorded in several places, including Deuteronomy 23:24 and Numbers 6:3. Or, the fruit can be dried to make raisins. Both raisins and wine are ways to preserve the nutrition of the grape for extended periods.

The surface of the grape berry contains a natural wax that traps wild yeast so that when the grapes are crushed and the juice expressed the agent of fermentation is present. Wine can be stored indefinitely; there are numerous records of amphorae of wine recovered from ships sunk in the Mediterranean thousands of years ago. A by-product of wine is vinegar (mentioned in Numbers 6:3; Ruth 2:14; Psalms 69:21; Proverbs 10:26; 25:20; Matthew 27:48; Mark 15:36; Luke 23:36; and John 19:29), which results from bacterial fermentation of wine.

One of the lesser-known uses of the grape is for the unripe fruits, which are very sour, as noted in Jeremiah 31:29 and Ezekiel 18:2, both of which apparently refer to the same proverb: "Why do you quote this proverb concerning the land of Israel: 'The parents have eaten sour grapes, but their children's mouths pucker at the taste'?" (NLT). Arab villagers regularly use the unripe grapes to make a seasoning. The grapes (red and green varieties are both used) are harvested when the berries are about 1 inch (0.75 cm) in diameter. These are dried and then finely ground. One of the common methods is mixing the grape powder with salt, pepper, and hyssop. (See Hyssop.) This mixture is then added to meat and vegetable dishes to impart a pleasantly sour taste. Green, that is unripe, grapes are also mentioned in Job 15:33, but in reference to destruction of the developing harvest.

Lastly, the utter uselessness of the wood of the vine is referred to in Ezekiel 15: "Son of man, how is the wood of a vine better than that of a branch on any of the trees in the forest?" (v. 2 NIV).

Figure 1. Traditional grape culture without a trellis. Vicinity of Suwaida, Syria.

Figure 2. Grapevines growing over a wall near Lebrak, Syria in June.

Figure 3. Trellis-grown grapes. Kufur Sumei, Galilee, Israel.

Figure 4. Green (i.e., unripe) grapes at stage for harvesting for preparation of condiment. Chios, Greece.

Figure 5. Pruning grapes in Cana, Galilee, Israel.

GRASS

Moldenke and Moldenke, among other Bible plant students, point out that in the Old Testament three very general types of vegetation are recognized: grass, herbs (larger plants), and trees.[1] The distinction among these is not sharp, they are literary, not scientific, conventions. Botanically, grass refers to a member of the grass family,[2] which includes major crops as maize, wheat, barley, sorghum, rice, and millet, as well as pasture and lawn grasses. The word translated as grass in the Bible, however, includes more than true grasses, what would commonly be referred to as herbaceous (i.e., non woody) native vegetation.

Many grasses are native to the Middle East, some forming a very important component of fodder in grazing lands. Because rainfall is unimodal in that part of the world, there is a flush of growth, the grasses and other plants flourish, but then most of them die back so that within as little as two months there is little green remaining.

This transitory growth is referred to in several scriptures as a picture of the fleeting nature of human life, as in 1 Peter 1:24 ("As the Scriptures say, 'People are like grass; their beauty is like a flower in the field. The grass withers and the flower fades'" NLT. Peter is quoting Isaiah 40:6).

A comparison that is less clear for present-day readers involves the grass on the rooftops, an image in 2 Kings 9:26: "while their inhabitants, shorn of strength, are dismayed and confounded, and have become like plants of the field and like tender grass, like grass on the housetops, blighted before it is grown" (ESV). See too Psalm 129:6 and Isaiah 37:27. The characteristic mud and wattle construction allows for roofs to support grass and other rapidly growing plants, all of which soon wither and die. This would be a familiar scene to the original recipients of the Bible.

---

1. Moldenke and Moldenke, Bible Plants.
2. Poaceae or Gramineae.

Figure 1. Bulbous meadow-grass,[3] a common grass in the Middle East. Tannourine, Mount Lebanon in April.

Figure 2. Bulbous meadow grass in late May. Sair, near Hebron, Palestinian Territory.

3. *Poa bulbosa*. This is a common grass with some strains that produce seedlings rather than grains, enabling an early establishment in the spring.

Figure 3. Verdant meadow with grass and anemones in spring, Hazar Merd, Sulaimani Province, Kurdish Iraq.

Figure 4. Rooftop in late spring. The weedy grasses have already shed their grains. Chios, Greece.

GUM

Mastic is a gum produced by incising the bark of the mastic tree and has long been used as a masticatory, an ingredient in medicines, and for the compounding of incense. So, it is not surprising that the home of Joakim, Susanna's husband, should have a mastic tree (Susanna/Daniel 13:54).

The finest mastic comes from the Greek island of Chios where a recognized variety occurs.[1] It is still an important crop on that island. Like other members of the genus, mastic has male and female trees. Only the male trees are used for gum production. Trees have been selected for the quality and quantity of gum production and are planted in plantations. Stems are incised in July and the harvest of the exuded, dried gum is finished in October.

While they do not produce the quality of gum of their Chios congeners, mastic trees[2] are common in the drier regions of the Mediterranean hills. Like the mastic gum trees, they are small in stature with spreading branches. The branches that were collected and burned to evict the refugees in the tower in Shechem could have been mastic (pine, also highly flammable, is present in that region): "All the people also cut down each one his branch and followed Abimelech, and put them on the inner chamber and set the inner chamber on fire over those inside, so that all the men of the tower of Shechem also died, about a thousand men and women" (Judges 9:49 NIV). Because of the oil in the leaves, mastic burns readily, one of the adaptations to a fire-maintained ecosystem.

The plant that produced the product rendered gum in Genesis 37:25 (the cargo of the Ishmaelites who would carry Joseph to Egypt) and Genesis 43:11 (the gift that Jacob sent to the Egyptian ruler) is not clear. It has been various translated as spicery (ASV, KJV), aromatic gum (NASB), and gum (ESV, NLT). A parsimonious explanation is that it is simply gum from the mastic tree, which is common in the region. I think it is unlikely, though not impossible, that it is gum derived from

---

1. *Pistacia lentiscus* var. *chia*.
2. *Pistacia lentiscus* var. *lentiscus*.

a gum-bearing species of milkvetch.³ These are more abundant further east in Iraq and Iran. (See Balm of Gilead.)

Figure 1. Mastic orchard, Chios, Greece.

Figure 2. Mastic gum. While related species and varieties of terebinths yield a usable gum, the highest quality comes from Chios, as it did in ancient times.

3. Species of the genus *Astragalus*, one of the largest genera of plants reaching its greatest diversity in Western Asia. Also known in North American as locoweed.

HENNA

"While the king was on his couch, my nard gave forth its fragrance. My beloved is to me a sachet of myrrh that lies between my breasts. My beloved is to me a cluster of henna[1] blossoms in the vineyards of Engedi" (Song of Songs 1:14 ESV).[2] Solomon's Song is a book redolent with plant fragrances. Clearly, the reference here is to the strong, very fragrant henna flowers that were used to prepare perfumes in ancient times.[3]

Some translators have suggested that the Hebrew *kopher* should be translated as camphor rather than henna. Camphor is a compound found in many plants and usually extracted from a relative of cinnamon.[4] While there may be some philological basis for considering camphor, the evidence from ethnobotany is overwhelming. Henna has been a part of Middle East culture since time immemorial; on the other hand, camphor has not and, further, the association of the source with Engedi in Song of Songs does not support the camphor tree.

Today, henna is best known as a coloring agent for hair treatments and widely used in many countries of Asia to ornament hands and feet for weddings. In this verse, however, reference is to the wonderful fragrance of the henna blossoms, a fitting climax to the well-known fragrances of nard and myrrh. The location of Engedi, at the edge of the Rift Valley, with its subtropical climate, is significant because henna is native to tropical and subtropical regions of Africa though now widely grown in other regions that do not experience freezing temperatures.

Henna is a many-branched shrub seldom over 18 feet (3 meters) tall with small, opposite leaves and creamy white flowers that can be borne almost any time of year. It is the leaves that are used to prepare the henna dye after they are dried, ground, and mixed with water. Its tolerance for

1. *Lawsonia inermis.*
2. The KJV, alone among the English translations I have seen, translates this as "camphire," camphor. Camphor is produced by a diversity of unrelated plants and is a valued and widely used medicine and fumigant. No doubt it was known in Bible days. However, the flowers of the chief source of camphor, *Cinnamomum camphora,* have little fragrance compared to henna.
3. Renaut, *Henna Perfume,* 194.
4. Lemmelijn, *Flora Canticorum,* 43.

saline soils is what makes it a suitable planting in desert oases where it is frequently found as a border in date palm plantations.

Song of Songs 1:14 is the only reference to henna in the Bible and only refers to the fragrance of the flowers. In the United States, henna is a common component of cosmetics and widely used in body art. It is very likely that ancients in the Holy Land used henna much as it is used today. While most of the world's henna production is used in India, north Africa, and the Middle East for body art, it has several medical applications. Henna binds with keratin in the skin and hair, providing protection against infection as well as being an effective sunscreen.[5]

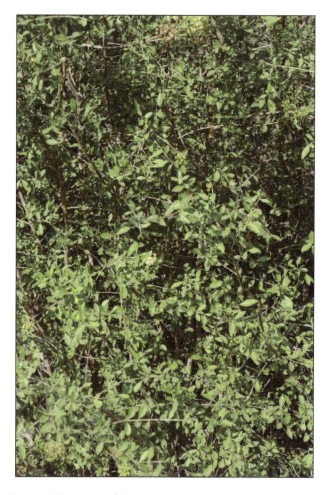

Figure 1. Henna, Masah Oasis, Hajjar Mountains, northern Oman.

5. Bodoni Semwal et al., *Henna*, 85.

Figure 2. A cluster of henna flowers. They have a heavy, sweet fragrance.

Figure 3. Henna leaves are powdered for use. The cosmetic is available throughout Western Asia. Iran is the biggest producer.

154 HENNA

Figure 4. Henna is typically used to decorate brides. The general rule is: the closer relation to the bride, the more henna. Wedding in Khartoum, Sudan.

HYSSOP

Hyssop[1] *is one of* the better-known plants of the Bible, referred to in ten places in the Old Testament and two in the New. This plant, or a product of this plant, formed an important part of the Passover (Exodus 12:22), ceremonial cleansing from skin disease (Leviticus 14), and the red heifer offering (Numbers 19). It is perhaps in reference to the latter that David mentions hyssop in Psalm 51:7 in the well-known prayer of confession ("Purge me with hyssop, and I shall be clean: wash me, and I shall be whiter than snow" KJV).

The New Testament reference is in John 19:29 (discussed below). Hebrews 9:19 refers to the ceremonial cleansing of the children of Israel and the use of hyssop, though this use is not mentioned in the Old Testament. The remaining reference, 1 Kings 4:33, is the only Old Testament verse that does not mention hyssop in a ceremonial use. It is also one of the most puzzling verses dealing with this plant.

Hyssop must have the following features, according to the scriptures where it is mentioned. It should grow on a "wall" (1 Kings 4:33). The plant and/or its extracts should be useful for purgatives. In both Leviticus 14 and Numbers 19, hyssop is associated with cedar wood implying a purgative use. Moreover, it may have been commercially available perhaps in the same way it is today (see discussion below). This could explain the use of the plant by the children of Israel in the Nile Delta prior to their departure from Egypt, where it does not occur, though it has been found in Sinai.[2] There are no archeological finds of hyssop from ancient Egypt (though it does appear in the Roman era and later) raising the question of how the children of Israel first encountered its use.

For all of these uses, Syrian hyssop—a relative of the well-known kitchen herbs oregano and marjoram—seems the most likely candidate.

Yet, some modern Bible scholars still express uncertainty about the actual identity of the plant named 'ēzôb in Hebrew (usually translated hyssop) and some suggest that it could be caper,[3] a very common shrub in the

---

1. *Origanum syriacum*. An older name is *O. maru* or rarely, *Majorana syriaca.*.
2. Boulos, *Flora of Egypt*, 12.
3. *Capparis spinosa*.

Middle East.[4] The only evidence for this is the verse in 1 Kings 4:33 referring to hyssop growing from a wall. This has often been assumed to be a masonry wall, like those commonly seen in the older parts of cities in the Middle East where caper is very common. The issue is that this description does not apply to hyssop, as it never grows out of stone walls. To suggest, however, that Solomon was thinking of caper only complicates the matter as there is a different word for caper in Hebrew. A further problem with caper is how it is used. The fruit, a soft berry-like structure when mature, was apparently used as an aphrodisiac. The fruits would have to be dried—certainly a messy, tedious if not impossible task. Lastly, Palestinians I have interviewed never use any part of the caper plant for food or condiment.

Just the opposite is true of hyssop, known in Arabic as *za'atar* and one of the most widely used and valued herbs in the Middle East. A typical Arab breakfast is bread dipped in olive oil and *za'atar*. It is available in dried form in almost any Arab market as a mixture of hyssop, sesame seeds, salt, and sometimes olive oil and other ingredients. The flavor is rather like that of a pizza. I asked the Samaritans, native Arabic speakers, on Mount Gerizim which plant they use for sprinkling in their Passover rites, and their answer was *za'atar*.[5] This confirms earlier observations.[6]

In 1 Kings 4:33 it seems at first look that the plant in question cannot be hyssop, as this does not grow out of a stone wall, which caper does; but in other references not the slightest doubt can exist as to the plant's identity as hyssop and by no stretch of imagination could caper be meant. Let's look at the text. "He spoke of trees, from the cedar that is in Lebanon to the hyssop that grows out of the wall. He spoke also of beasts, and of birds, and of reptiles, and of fish." The Hebrew word *qîr* used in 1 Kings 4:33 is the word frequently used for wall (e.g., Leviticus 14:37; 1 Kings 6:5, and many other places), but this use does not preclude reference to natural ledges such as are common in the mountains. In this verse, Solomon is speaking of natural history, not manmade objects, so that reference to a masonry wall could be out of context. Indeed, hyssop is most frequent on rocky ledges and outcrops in the mountains, rock formations that can accurately be described as wall-like.[7]

---

4. Moldenke and Moldenke, *Bible Plants*, 161–62. Their treatment is a good overview of the history of translation of hyssop.

5. Unbeknownst to me at the time, Crowfoot and Baldensperger (*Hyssop*) had interviewed the Samaritan High Priest who said hyssop was used. But unlike me, they witnessed the actual sprinkling of the blood of the Passover and noted that dried plants were not used.

6. Crowfoot and Baldensperger, *Palestine Hyssop*, 90–91.

7. For the suggestion that rocky ledges might be intended I am thankful to the Dutch theologian Henk Medema.

One final problem in the identity of hyssop remains and that is in John 19:29 ("A jar of wine vinegar was there, so they soaked a sponge in it, put the sponge on a stalk of the hyssop plant, and lifted it to Jesus' lips" NIV). The word here is the same as that in Hebrews 9:19 and there seems little doubt that hyssop is meant. How the hyssop was used is the problem. There are two possibilities. The first is that the sponge was put on a long stalk of the hyssop plant. But this is unlikely due to the small stature of hyssop; it would nearly be impossible to find a stem more than a meter long and even then, the stem often branches. Alternatively, the Greek words meaning "binding it to hyssop" might also suggest that the hyssop plant was a kind of holder for the sponge. This is plausible because of the growth habit of the hyssop where a sponge could be put in the center of the much-branched plant. Why this would be necessary is unclear.

Figure 1. Hyssop growing out of a "wall" in northern Syria.

Figure 2. Hyssop ready for drying.

Figure 3. Collecting hyssop in the rocky hills near Kufur Yusef, Galilee, Israel.

Figure 4. The main ingredient of the very popular spice *zaatar* is hyssop. Spice market, Straight Street, Damascus.

Hyssop, then, was used for its value in worship in Bible times rather than in the manner it is now, as a widely consumed herb. It is another example of a member of the native flora finding place in the Scriptures as well as kitchens of today. In fact, the hyssop business is flourishing in no small measure because of its purported medicinal uses.[8]

---

8. Uses well summarized in Abu Alwafa, *Raw to Go*. Za'atar has become increasingly popular so that collecting in the wild cannot meet the demand. Its medical uses are legion, enhanced by the aura of being cited in sacred texts.

JUNIPER

Juniper is a group of trees that is sometimes conflated with the junipers[1] and is represented in the Levant by three or four species, which can reach a size suitable for timber. Prickly juniper[2] and Greek juniper[3] grow at higher elevations (along with the less frequent Syrian juniper)[4] while Phoenician juniper[5] is common in drier regions. The latter has been found in archeological sites in southern Israel.[6]

Cypress, like cedar of Lebanon, has inspired numerous, though misapplied, common names. It was one of the most important and durable timber trees in the ancient eastern Mediterranean world.

Figure 1. Near the summit of Mount Lebanon. The fog is typical and essential for the native vegetation in a region of low rainfall. The trees in the foreground are a mixture of Greek juniper and Cilician fir.

1. Species of the genus *Juniperus*.
2. *Juniperus oxycedrus*.
3. *Juniperus excelsa*.
4. *Juniperus drupacea*.
5. *Juniperus phoenicea*.
6. Liphschitz, *Masada Timber*.

Figure 2. Greek juniper, Qammouaa, northern Lebanon.

Figure 3. Cilician fir. Qammouaa, northern Lebanon.

LADANUM

What is the balm in the cargo that Ishmaelites were taking to Egypt in Genesis 37:25? The Hebrew word *tsorî* is regularly translated as myrrh (ASV), with only the Darby translation using ladanum. However, a different word, *môr*, is normally used for myrrh. The fact that the caravan is specifically stated as coming from Gilead suggests that the product is from Gilead, though, of course, it could have been transshipped from elsewhere.

Later, in Genesis 43:11 Jacob specifically states that this (*tsorî*) is one of the "best products of the land" (NIV) clearly suggesting it was a local product.[1] In the Levant there are two species of rockrose, pink rock rose[2] and sageleaf rock rose.[3] The former is widespread around the Mediterranean.

Species of rock rose are attractive, small shrubs adapted to fire-maintained ecosystems. The flowers are large and showy, either pink or white. Volatile, fragrant compounds are produced in specialized hairs that cover most of the plant.

Pink rock rose has been harvested for millennia for its resin which is used both as a medicine and to compound perfume. There is considerable interest in its use for skin diseases and other ailments. In English, the resin of the pink rock rose is known as ladanum (not to be confused with laudanum, a tincture of opium popular in the Victorian era).

I believe that the balm of Gilead is derived from the pink rock rose. As I argue in the treatment of myrrh, there is little support for myrrh being grown in Gilead.

One of the features of the genus is the presence of resins and oils, producing a fragrance with an overtone of turpentine. The source of our English word turpentine is derived from the word terebinth. In North America, turpentine is derived from pine trees but in ancient times terebinth was the source of a compound used in a similar manner. The resin of this tree is a candidate for the famed balm of Gilead (Jeremiah 8:22).

---

1. Jacob mentions myrrh in the verse, indicating that myrrh, though not indigenous, was available in Gilead.
2. *Cistus creticus.*
3. *Cistus salvifolius.* Also known as white rock rose.

Because of the attractive imagery of the reference in Jeremiah 8:22, balm of Gilead has entered American English in a variety of ways. One of the most interesting to me is in the naming of plants.[4] A widespread species of poplar called balm of Gilead[5] is common in the northern United States, Canada, and Alaska, the resinous sticky buds having a strong, fragrant odor. In fact, on a hot day this odor fills the summer air. This product is still available, compounded as a salve, and linked with the biblical reference.

Another possible source for the true balm of Gilead is mastic.[6] The first mention of this balm is associated with the story of Joseph. Rather than kill Joseph, his brothers sold him to "a caravan of Ishmaelites coming from Gilead. Their camels were loaded with spices, balm (*tsorî*), and myrrh, and they were on their way to take them down to Egypt" (Genesis 37:25). "Is there no balm (*tsorî*) in Gilead?" asks the weeping prophet in Jeremiah 8:22. The same word, *tsorî*, is used in Jeremiah 46:11, 51:8, and Ezekiel 27:17. In all these verses mastic fits well.

This resin is now known to be one of the materials used in preparation of mummies in ancient Egypt.[7] Since terebinth trees are not native to Egypt, resin was imported from Gilead and contiguous regions.

The small, hard fruits of Palestine terebinth are sold in Arab markets as a condiment and are sometimes a component of *zaatar*, a spicy mix put on hot bread. The flavor reminds me of pine resin.

The appellation of balm to the exudate of these trees is appropriate since they have been used as medicine since time immemorial and at present terebinth preparations are being studied for their medical efficacy.[8]

---

4. Species of the genus *Populus*. In parts of the southern United States the unrelated *Liriodendron tulipifera* is commonly called yellow poplar.
5. *Populus gileadensis*.
6. *Pistacia lentiscus*.
7. Buckley and Evershed, *Embalming Agents*.
8. Milia et al., *Preparations of Pistacia*.

Figure 1. Pink rock rose showing the abundant glandular hairs that are the source of the resin. Mountains west of Hamah, Syria.

Figure 2. Pink rock rose, Dibeen Forest, Jordan.

Figure 3. Sageleaf rockrose, Lebanon.

Figure 4. Fruits of the two rockrose species. On the right is pink rock rose with the distinctive glandular hairs. Left are the fruits of sage leaf rock rose.

LAUREL

Laurel[1] *was used to* crown winners in ancient games. It remains a winner today, but in a different way. In an American home the crowning use of the laurel is still for its leaves, known as bay leaves—not for honor but to give an aromatic flavor when preparing Mediterranean dishes.

Two types of crowns are mentioned in the New Testament. The first is a regal crown of precious metal, what we would normally think of as a royal crown with gold and studded with jewels. The second is the laurel wreath, presented to the winner of the ancient games. The symbolism of this prize would be well known to New Testament writers acquainted with Greek culture. A kind of vegetable tiara, it was woven from the leaves and young branches of the laurel. A literal translation of the Latin name is the noble laurel, a very apt description of this shrub or small tree common in forest communities throughout the Mediterranean region. Laurel is one of the few plants mentioned solely in the New Testament.

Paul the apostle was influenced by Greek culture. He implies the laurel wreath of the Greek games in three epistles. The image is especially clear in 2 Timothy 2:5, where a "victor's crown" is mentioned. Similarly, other apostles mention this. In 1 Peter 5:4 a non-fading crown is contrasted with a fading (i.e., laurel) crown. James suggests a laurel crown for those who persevere (James 1:12).

Laurel is a shrub or small tree with evergreen, leathery leaves. Like its relative sassafras, laurel is perfused with an aromatic oil. Flowers are greenish, small, and appear in the spring. Shiny black fleshy fruits are produced in October or November

Best known as the bay leaves of cooking, laurel was used as an ornament in Greek culture and is mentioned only in the New Testament. The tradition of laurel lives on in our language in such words as laurel, laureate, and baccalaureate.

1. *Laurus nobilis.*

Figure 1. Laurel tree in Rome.

Figure 2. Flowers in early spring. Chouf, Mount Lebanon.

Figure 3. Fruiting laurel near Kufur Sumei, Galilee, Israel.

Figure 4. Reverse side of US dime with laurel on left, and oak on right. United State coinage has featured laurel since the birth of the nation.

LEEKS

Plants mentioned as foods in the Bible are still widely used in Western Asia. Unique to the wilderness experience are five vegetables well known today: cucumbers, melons, leeks, onions, and garlic (Numbers 11:5). Anyone who has spent time in the Middle East is aware how much all of these are relished—even essential—except for leeks. This plant is seldom grown in the Middle East. It is available in larger cities but is purchased chiefly by foreigners and thus does not have the legacy of use of other ancient crops. On the other hand, a crop grown only in the Delta region of Egypt, known in Arabic as *kurrat*,[1] is a well known albeit minor crop.

The differences between the widely grown vegetable garden leek[2] and the leek grown in Egypt is the smaller size of *kurrat* and the absence of the garden leek's longer stem with a pronounced bulbous base. Garden leek is grown mainly for its white stems while *kurrat* is grown for its leaves.

Remains of *kurrat* have been found at archeological sites indicating selection for this leafy type of leek from ancient times.[3] However, this species or cultivar of leek was not formally named until 1926 when K. Krause of the Dahlem Botanical Garden in Berlin found a leek flowering that had been grown from seeds collected by George Schweinfurth (1836–1925), who had spent many years botanizing in Egypt and Sudan.

Modern use of *kurrat* is in green salads and as a component of *tameeah*, the traditional fried cakes of broad beans popular in Egypt and Sudan. The leaves are not as stringy as those of garden leek (which traditionally are not eaten) but have a strong flavor.

Most English-speaking readers of the "vegetable list" in Numbers 11 envision the leeks mentioned there as the stout plants with a long white stem sold in grocery stores. The leeks in the Bible, however, were much shorter and lacked the larger stem.

1. *Allium kurrat.*
2. *Allium porrum.*
3. Murray, *Egypt Condiments*, 630.

Figure 1. Field of *kurrat* near Alexandria, Egypt, ready for harvest.

Figure 2. The tender leaves are cut and tied into bundles with cordage made from palm leaves.

LENTIL

Lentils, as in Bible days, are one of the most important crops in the modern Middle East. Despite their widespread planting and use in a variety of dishes, lentils are mentioned just a few times in the Bible.

Although Genesis 25:30, 34; 2 Samuel 17:28; 23:12, and Ezekiel 4:9 are the only references to this legume crop in the Bible, it is certain that lentils[1] were widely planted and utilized during the time the Bible was written. In fact, lentils are native to the Middle East and have been part of the guild of crops cultivated for almost ten millennia. Little work has been done on the history of their domestication, unlike the voluminous research on the grains wheat and barley.[2] Today, lentils are extensively grown and an important source of protein. Like many other legumes, lentils are rich in essential amino acids so are a good supplement to a low-protein diet.

Lentil plants are low growing, delicate annuals, with small white or bluish flowers. They are planted in the winter and are harvested in late spring or early summer, a cropping system linked with barley and wheat. One of the most interesting things about the culture of lentils is that they are often grown in very small patches. It is not uncommon to see a patch of lentils only a few yards in diameter among olive trees or on a ledge in the mountains.

Both lentil and barley are often taken to the same threshing floors because they ripen at the same time. These threshing floors appear little changed since Bible days with large flat rocks, worn smooth by centuries of threshing and surrounded by stone walls.

There are two main types of lentils. One is a large, dark lentil, eaten without the seed coat being removed. The second is a small lentil with red cotyledons and a thick seed coat. This is usually prepared by grinding off the outer layer, the seed coat, leaving the red cotyledons. The seed coat residue is fed to animals. Lentils of this type cook more rapidly.[3]

1. *Lens culinaris.*
2. Liber et al., *History of Lentil.*
3. Cooking of food in Bible times needs to be emphasized because most would be done with charcoal. Collecting the wood, preparing the charcoal or purchasing it added effort and expense to cooking. That is no doubt why crops such as hard-seeded lentils were treated to require less cooking time. The same may be true of *frikeh* and other food products.

In the account in Genesis 25, Jacob trades the humble lentil stew for Esau's birth right. For this reason Esau is called Edom ("red").

Figure 1. A small patch of lentils in an olive grove near Nablus, Palestinian Territories.

Figure 2. Lentils ready for threshing at a threshing floor east of Bethlehem.

LENTIL 177

Figure 3. Lentils ready for harvest. Tel Hadya, Syria.

Figure 4. The source of the familiar red lentils is a hard seeded variety with the seed coat removed. I have chipped a few seeds to show the pink cotyledons.

LILIES

> *"In the beauty of the lilies Christ was born across the sea,*
> *With a glory in his bosom that transfigures you and me."*

These words from the well-known American hymn, The Battle Hymn of the Republic,[1] reflect the readily recognized (by a then Bible-literate society) image of the lily in Scripture. The tradition lives on, hundreds of churches are called Lily of the Valley or Rose of Sharon. But the Hebrew word translated lily is applied to a disparate group of plants, all with attractive flowers. Historical treatments of the plant purported to be the lily are reviewed elsewhere.[2] There is controversy among Bible scholars as summarized, for example by Kitto[3] and Zohary.[4]

Here I treat those plants which in most English translations are rendered lily.

White Lily

Considering the features of the lily in the three occurrences in the Old Testament, that is, in the design of the temple of Solomon; in the gardens of Song of Songs; and as a beautiful plant in the restored Israel in Hosea, the plant needs the following features. It should have some semblance to the brim of a cup, be stylized as in the carving on the chapiters of the pillars Jachin and Boaz. Based on these references alone, it would be difficult to speak to the botanical determination of the plant and for some time I considered the inclusion of the white lily as an unlikely flower in the flora of Scripture. However, there are images on ancient pillars and coins from

---

1. Written by Julia Ward Howe in 1861.
2. Moldenke and Moldenke, *Plants of the Bible*, 120.
3. Royle, *Biblical Literature*, 250–51.
4. Zohary, *Plants*, 176. "The biblical Hebrew term, *shoshan* (*shushan*) is certainly the white (true) lily, despite the massive literature and the furious debate among linguists as to its identification. The white lily grows in Galilee on Mt. Carmel and was once more common in the Holy Land." Zohary does not document its prior distribution nor document records of large populations in other paces that it grows outside the Holy Land.

Judea that botanically could be nothing but the Easter lily.[5] It is not a common plant and in Israel grows only on rocky slopes in the northern part of the country, though it has a wide range around the Mediterranean.[6] Because of its presence in habitats often difficult to access and due to its rarity it would be less familiar than the other plants translated as "lily." Its beauty and relative ease of cultivation from bulbs has led to widespread collection from nature. Interestingly, the German physician cum botanist and plant explorer Leonhard Rauwolf (1535?-96) reported lilies being sold in bouquets in the market in Aleppo, Syria. Assuming this practice was widespread, this activity could lead to a diminution of populations, but I find no documentation that it was once as widespread as reported.[7]

Another pair of plants have been suggested as the lily in the Song of Solomon—lotus and blue water lily.[8] Because there is little evidence for lotus in the Levant, and since the blue water lily's presence and iconography in Egypt is well documented, I favor the water lily.

In Solomon's love poem there is a hint of fragrance (Song of Songs 5:13, "His cheeks are like beds of spice yielding perfume. His lips are like lilies dripping with myrrh" NIV). In Hosea 14:5, the imagery is of a restored, fruitful Israel. It is not clear which plant is intended, perhaps tulip.

Lilies of the Field

"And why are you anxious about clothing? Consider the lilies of the field, how they grow: they neither toil nor spin" (Luke 12:27 ESV). Jesus' famous words about the lilies, with characteristic semitic hyperbole, compares the beauty of these wildflowers to that of the most resplendent king of Israel, Solomon. I believe this to be the common anemone,[9] with its striking large flowers that are usually bright red but occasionally in white or bluish hues.

---

5. Meshorer, *Ancient Coinage*, 62–63. Though stylized, I have little doubt that the images on these are the white lily, the well-known Easter lily, *Lilium candidum*.

6. Zaccai et al., *Israel Lily*, 297–88.

7. Walter et al., *Emperor's Herbarium*, 8. The work of Rauwolf included preparing pressed, dried herbarium Specimens to document his collection, which is still extant. Among the specimens are those of *Lilium candidum*.

8. Suderman, *Lotus Versus Lily*. Suderman bases his argument that lily in Song of Solomon is *Nymphaea caerulea*, noting its use in Mesopotamian civilization, indicating its widespread use was assimilated by ancient Israel. I agree with Koops (*Each According to Its Kind*, 166–67) that the words translated lily are general terms for attractive flowers.

9. *Anemone coronaria*. Among various other common names is poppy anemone because of the resemblance of the red form of this species to the common field poppy, *Papaver rhoeas*. See field poppy.

The association of this plant with Jesus' ministry seems likely because the setting of Jesus' teaching suggests wildflowers such as anemones were nearby. These often occur in large populations on hillsides where Jesus' audiences met. I think this makes it unlikely that the flower Jesus referred to was the narcissus (see below), which favors wetter areas where a crowd would be unlikely to gather, especially if they sat on the ground. The scientific name of the anemone refers to a crown, appropriate considering Jesus' reference to the regal glory of King Solomon.

Lily of the Valley

A prime candidate is a species of narcissus[10] that is widely distributed from the Maghreb to the Zagros Mountains and around the Mediterranean. The intensely fragrant white and yellow flowers appear in the spring, coinciding with the vernal equinox. Narcissus is therefore a symbol of Newroz, a celebration of the Spring equinox in several west Asian countries. Thus, the symbolism of narcissus has an ancient tradition. After flowering, the leaves wither and little is left by summer to mark its presence.

The present-day abundance of the narcissus is diminished, like that of many other segetal (weeds growing with crops) species that disappeared with the advent of deep, machine plowing in contrast to the traditional shallower plowing of draft animals, a form of cultivation allowing many of these plants to persist. This is especially true of plants that have underground storage organs—corms, bulbs, rhizomes—including tulips, narcissus, and gladiolus. Gentle, shallow plowing does not destroy these propagules and, in some cases, favors their growth. But when the soil is deep plowed, the organs are buried to a level from which they cannot emerge. At the same time there has been an alarming degradation of the environment through development and expansion of agriculture. As a result of widespread habitat destruction, the vast fields of narcissus are less common in the Middle East.

What about Water Lilies?

Some have suggested that the lily motif used, for example, in the capitols of the pillars Jachin and Boaz are stylized water lilies,[11] frequent in ancient Egyp-

---

10. *Narcissus tazetta*. There are numerous common names.

11. *Nymphaea nouchali* is the correct name for this famous fragrant blue water lily but an older name, *N. caerulea*, is widely ensconced in the literature.

tian art, which was imbibed by Assyria and Israel.[12] While these obligately wetland plants can't be ruled out, I favor considering the autochthonous species as they would be most familiar to the original recipients of the Scriptures.

Figure 1. Easter lily in my garden.

Figure 2. Crown anemone. Near Suaida, Syria.

12. MacDonald, *Lotus Symbolism*. Considerable clarification would obtain if the author had explained that the common name "lotus" is regularly applied to unrelated plants in the genus *Nelumbo* (and a diversity of other non-water lilies) and used the more suitable common name of "water lily." The pink-flowered *N. nucifera* is widely figured in Buddhist culture and is usually referred to as "sacred lotus."

Figure 3. Field of crown anemone near Derbendikhan, Kurdish Iraq showing the purple-flowered variant.

Figure 4. I was a guest of a Kurdish university while doing field work in Kurdish Iraq and among many kindnesses was provided with armed guards. I love the dissonance of the automatic weapon with the narcissus. The yellow dots in the background are narcissus in a low, moist area. Above Dokan, Kurdish Iraq.

LILIES 183

Figure 5. The narcissus flower are as fragrant as they are attractive, Dokan.

Figure 6. Blue water lily. Komarov Botanical Institute, St. Petersburg.

MALLOW

What do "wild greens" and "mallow" have in common? Numerous plants in different parts of the world provide "wild greens." And as for mallows, this common name is usually associated with a group of wetland plants. So what is this plant and why is it translated in such disparate ways? The only reference is in Job, in a discourse that is a kind of tirade on Job's part, impugning those he views as judging them. Put another way, he considers these coarse vagabonds of little credibility or, in Job's own words, "a base and nameless brood." Strong language for men who apparently know how to survive in a tough environment.

Many plants have edible foliage, but few are large enough to provide a meaningful amount of food, especially in a desert. One of these is a common desert shrub translated "mallow" in the KJV (not to be confused with the wetland plants by that common name) in Job 30:3–4 and "salt herbs" in the NIV. "Haggard from want and hunger, they roamed the parched land in desolate wastelands at night. In the brush they gathered salt herbs, and their food was the root of the broom tree" (Job 30:3–4 NIV).

The much-branched, greyish-green shrub, translated mallow in the KJV, is associated with the desert plant broom. The precise identity of this food source is not clear, but it is likely saltbush,[1] a plant of desert or other saline areas. I have eaten the leaves, which possess salt-secreting glands, and found them pleasant. They are also an important food for camels.[2]

One modern translation, *The Message*, translates this as "chewing on old bones and licking old tin cans," eviscerating any botanical meaning from the text.

---

1. *Atriplex halimus*.

2. Walker et al. (*Atriplex halimus*, 116–18) review traditional uses as well as positing new uses.

Figure 1. The characteristic grey-green color of the foliage is obvious in this image taken at the International Center for Agricultural Research in the Dry Areas, Tel Hadya, Syria.

Figure 2. Salt crystals exudated by mallow leaves. Aqaba Bird Sancturary, Jordan.

MANDRAKE

Possibly no Bible plant is more mysterious than the mandrake,[1] known only in Genesis 30:14 and Song of Songs 7:13, although it is common throughout the Middle East and Europe. Mandrake is a member of the nightshade family that includes well known poisonous plants such as nightshade, jimsonweed, tobacco, and, paradoxically, some of the most common vegetables, such as potatoes, tomatoes, green pepper, and eggplants.

As the Bible so accurately describes (Genesis 30:14), the mandrake often grows as a weed in wheat fields. It has several large, wrinkled, dark green leaves that lie flat on the ground in a rosette. In the center of this rosette a cluster of attractive purple flowers appears in the winter. Flowers have airs that prevent the entry of water, an important adaptation for a bell-shaped upright flower that appears during the rainy season.

The fruits, as noted in Song of Songs 7:13 ("The mandrakes send out their fragrance, and at our door is every delicacy, both new and old, that I have stored up for you, my lover," NIV), are produced in the early summer and have a very attractive fragrance.[2] Arab friends warned me that it was toxic. On the other hand, Harrison states that local people eat it with impunity.[3] So, it was with some trepidation that I ate part of a ripe fruit. If it is poisonous, then the poison is either very weak or very slow acting as I felt no discomfort after tasting a bit. The taste? As I recall, it reminded me of the taste of ground cherry[4] with a sweet but insipid flavor. Mukaddasi describes its use as a fruit in Syria, rightly noting that the root is toxic.[5] It was a highly valued fruit in Egypt, where it was grown in royal gardens and "collected in armfuls."[6]

The root of the mandrake may be a meter long and weigh several kilograms. It has bizarre often human-like shapes and for this reason is highly regarded by the superstitious.

1. *Mandragora officinalis.*
2. Fleisher and Fleisher, *Mandrake Fragrance.*
3. Harrison, *Mandrake Ancient World,* 91.
4. Species of the genus *Physalis.*
5. Mukaddasi, *Description of Syria,* 71.
6. Bosse-Griffiths, *Mandrake Fruit,* 90.

Reuben was well advised to recommend the plant as a fertility drug. Recent research has shown that the plant has a rich diversity of drugs, including those that might aid in conception. In addition, there is a growing interest in the use of these plants known for millennia for their medical and cultic use.[7]

Figure 1. Mandrake just beginning to flower. Karak, Jordan.

Figure 2. Ripe fruits if mandrake. Wadi Addis, Amman, Jordan.

7. Waniakowa, *Two Magic Plants*. There are other similar reviews produced in the past several years.

MINT

Unlike dill and cumin, mint is a perennial plant. There are several species and hundreds of cultivars of mint, so it is not possible to state which species is included in the Bible. The mint family is especially well represented in the eastern Mediterranean and several of the native genera are used for teas and flavorings. The word translated mint could refer to several of these, including the widespread native mint, or spearmint.[1]

The native habitats for this species are moist places such as low marshy areas or margins of streams and irrigation ditches. The attractive pink flowers are borne in the spring. But it is the young and tender leaves that are used for flavoring. How they were used in Bible times is not indicated but present use in the Middle East includes flavoring yoghurt, added to black tea, and in salads. Because the vegetative portion is used, it is likely that mint was more widely used by lower-income people than dill and cumin as they require fruiting material.

Figure 1. Spearmint[2] at Ein Al Ouja spring, below Taybaya, Palestinian Territory.

1. *Mentha longifolia.*
2. *Mentha longifolia.*

Figure 2. Leaves of field mint,[3] Ourika, Morocco.

3. *Mentha arvensis*, tentative determination.

MUSTARD

Mustard. The first thing most Americans think of is a yellow container with a sauce essential for hot dogs. Mustard is one of the best-known condiments in the United States and at the same time is one of the best-known plants in the Bible and the Qu'ran. In both books it is a picture of something tiny, a measure of smallness. Further, in the New Testament it additionally represents something miniscule that can become a monstrous growth as well as a symbol of faith.

Jesus used mustard in his teaching. Through parables, he taught ordinary people. His examples were relevant, identifying with his audience through examples from everyday life. In the parable of the mustard (Matthew 13:31–33), it was apparent to Jesus' audience what he was talking about—they had asked questions about the parable of the tares, but not the mustard seed.

The three features of the mustard plant emphasized by Jesus are the small size of the seed, the large size of the plant in relation to the seed, and its implied rapid growth. What plant is the mustard mentioned in both the Qu'ran and the Bible?

The Greek word translated mustard is *sinapi*, (Matthew 13:31; 17:20; Mark 4:31; Luke 13:19; 17:6), and the Hebrew equivalent *chardal* (the modern Arabic cognate *khardal*). The Jewish tradition, however, states that it is not a garden vegetable, but that it is grown in fields. It has been suggested that toothbrush tree[1] is meant, as the Arabs call this tree *khardal*. But there are very strong arguments against this. First, toothbrush tree is a desert shrub. Second, it is never cultivated for food or forage, although I have seen camels grazing it. Third, it has a very restricted distribution in the Holy Land, being found only in deserts near the Dead Sea. Lastly, the fruits are large and would hardly fit the picture of being among the smallest of seeds, as the imagery intended by the parable. In fact, these would be larger than anything planted in a garden. Moldenke and Moldenke provide a helpful summary of reasons why toothbrush tree cannot be *sinapi*.[2] Therefore,

---

1. *Salvadora persica*. Segments of young stems have traditionally been used to clean teeth, hence the common name.
2. Moldenke and Moldenke, *Bible Plants*, 220–21.

the most likely plants are herbaceous members of the mustard family, the Brassicaceae.

Candidates are the black mustard[3] and the white mustard.[4] Their seeds are around about 1–3 mm in diameter and they can grow to a height of between 1 and 3.5 meters. Mustards have edible leaves and, after cooking, the taste is pleasant and the pungency reduced. All mustards have small seeds and are characterized by rapid germination and seedling growth, annual habit, and spring flowering.

Though there is no record of mustard cultivation in the ancient Middle East, the culture of true mustards[5] in Bible times cannot be totally ruled out. Modern commercial mustard is prepared by grinding the seeds of black and white mustard and mixing them together—a practice unknown even to this day in Bible lands.

For reasons inexplicable, arugula,[6] also known as rocket, has never been posited as the mustard of the Bible. Yet it is native to the region and widely cultivated. In the United States it has become increasingly popular in upscale salad mixes and is easy to grow in a variety of soils and climatic conditions. Seeds are smaller than true mustards. Germination is rapid and after a few months the plants reach a height of 1 meter (3 feet). I do not consider this small size a difficulty in exegesis in the parable of the mustard plant growing to an enormous size because Jesus is using hyperbole and simply emphasizing the striking contrast between the small size of the seed *relative to* the fully grown plant.

Zohary suggests that arugula was the "herbs" sought by Elisha's disciples near Gilgal, which is in the Jordan Valley (2 Kings 4:38–39).[7] My observations support this because I have collected colycinth fruits in early March when the fields around Gilgal were covered with arugula.

From my interviews of farmers, I learned that the vegetative portions of wild relatives of mustard are collected in the early spring and relished as a cooked vegetable. Perhaps the leaves were used as a vegetable like many members of the mustard family, a family including such well-known plants as cabbage, turnips, and broccoli. Yet certainty evades us when seeking to identify biblical mustard.

---

3. *Brassica nigra.*
4. *Sinapis arvense.* A synonym is *Brassica alba.*
5. Species of the genus *Brassica.*
6. *Eruca sativa.*
7. Zohary, *Plants,* 101.

Recent archaeological work in Iran found that a native plant, Syrian mustard,[8] was harvested for fuel, but there is no evidence of growing true mustards.

Reflecting on the identity of the biblical mustard requires consideration of the literary style of the parables. They are filled with semitic hyperbole. In Matthew 13 the emphasis is on small things that become unusually large. This theme pervades all the parables: a sower sows a small seed, the enemy introduces tiny germs of evil, a minute lump of leaven permeates the whole loaf, an invisible treasure turns out to be the real value of a piece of ground, one very precious pearl is worth more than all the possessions of a merchant, an invisible net is drawn through the depths of the sea, and a scribe discovers things hitherto unseen in his treasure. Things that seem small, inconspicuous, hardly worth observation, invisible, turn out to be by far the greatest things. The strangeness of the symbolism is just the point that Jesus makes. This guides our reflections insofar as it helps us to appreciate that we need not be looking for something that *literally* becomes the biggest tree.

In addition to the arborescent growth of a garden vegetable, the other image of the mustard in the New Testament is of a small seed with great potential. In the picture, faith as small as a mustard seed enables one to move a mountain or large tree. In addition to the size differential, another feature of the mustard seed is the rapid germination. Seeds of any of these will begin germination within a few hours. While this application has not previously been made, I wonder if this seed behavior is not one of the reasons Jesus refers to the mustard seed.

The Qur'an includes similar imagery, that of mustard seed being a measure of the diminutive, "We shall fix the scales of justice on the Day of Resurrection, so that none will be wronged in the least; and even if it were equal to a mustard seed in weight We shall take it (into account)"(Sura 21:47 Ali). The only other reference is Sura 31 (The Wise), which also refers to the size of the mustard seed as a scale of what God sees.

---

8. Whitlam et al., *Cutting the Mustard*, 12–13.

Figure 1. Mustard on campus of Sulaimani University, Sulaimani, Kurdish Iraq.

Figure 2. Large fruiting mustard plants. Obviously, a bird cannot lodge in its branches per the parable in Matthew 13. Sair, near Hebron.

Figure 3. White mustard seed left, black mustard seed right.

MYRRH

Myrrh is the dried resin of several species of species of *Commiphora*. They are shrubs or small trees of the arid and semiarid regions of East and south Africa, Arabia, and the Indian subcontinent. Incisions in the bark allow the resin to exude, though sometimes there can be exudations without cutting. When it is dry it is collected and sold both for medicines and for incense. Recent work indicates that at least one species has opiate qualities.[1] This helps interpret Mark 15:23 where Jesus, on the cross, was offered vinegar mingled with myrrh but refused the drug. Myrrh, being a more widespread and diverse group of woody plants has more uses than Frankincense.

These two different myrrhs, medicinal and fragrant, are both translated from the same Hebrew word, *môr*. Odor of myrrh permeates the pages of Solomon's writings with more references than any other Bible author. Song of Solomon alone has seven references where its alluring fragrance is emphasized.

In the single reference in Proverbs 7, the adulterous woman refers to her bed as having been sprinkled with "myrrh, aloes, and cinnamon" (7:17). Myrrh is used in a similar way in Song of Solomon, that is, as a personal perfume with erotic overtones (5:5, 13). There is a guild of plants associated both with the adulterous woman in Proverbs as well as with the lovers in Song of Solomon. These include cassia, aloes, and myrrh. Myrrh is also linked with frankincense in other verses.

While these two fragrances are often cited together, they have different qualities. Frankincense, as the name implies, is more frequently used as an incense. The burning resin gives off an odor that reminds me of the fragrance of a pine tree. And frankincense is not used so much as a perfume, unlike myrrh.

Balm of Gilead?

The source of this fabled unguent and its preparation has been confused and treated variously by different authors. It has been described as a product of

---

1. Dolara, *Analgesic Effects*, 29.

myrrh, styrax, rock rose, terebinth, and no doubt other plants. An attempt to clarify the source adds information on fake balsams and argues that the original, true balm derives from the oriental sweetgum[2] producing storax.[3, 4]

If we accept the traditional location of Gilead, it is difficult to imagine suitable habitat for myrrh and indeed I have never seen it there. There remains considerable confusion among Bible commentaries and dictionaries about the identification of the plant known as balm or balm of Gilead in the Bible. Zohary[5] considers it a species of myrrh while Hepper,[6] correctly in my opinion, treats it as a species of rock rose.

Assuming myrrh is not indigenous in Gilead, it is reasonable that the myrrh was produced elsewhere. Since Gilead was not a recognized entrepôt, the Ishmaelite traders in Genesis 37 may simply had myrrh in their cargo. On the other hand, the product translated balm (*tsorî*) may have been derived from rock rose, which grows in a habitat much different than myrrh. The proverbial further research is needed.

Ancient writers described myrrh "trees" in Judea, which were extinct by the time of Christ. Analysis of the contents of powder boxes showed no myrrh (or frankincense) but a chemical that is a known component of labdanum.[7] While not conclusively documenting the balm of the Ishmaelite traders as rock rose, this discovery is evidence of the use of the resin, which would have to originate from a Mediterranean oak-pine vegetation characteristic of Gilead.

Balm of Gilead is a widely known plant product, though the extent of its recognition is not proportional to understanding what it really is, that is, the resin of a terebinth tree. Its appeal is well expressed in the spiritual:

> *There is a balm in Gilead*
> *To make the wounded whole;*
> *There is a balm in Gilead*
> *To heal the sin sick soul.*

---

2. *Liquidambar orientalis.* This tree is restricted in its distribution to southwestern Turkey, but also widely planted.
3. There are several other names for the product adding to the confusion.
4. Custódio and Velga-Junior, *True and Common Balsams*, 1375–76.
5. Zohary, *Plants*, 199.
6. Hepper, *Baker Encyclopedia*, 147. Hepper suggests that *Cistus salvifolius* is the source of the resin. It is *Cistus creticus* that produces the resin known as labdanum.
7. Ben-Yehoshua et al., *Ancient Spices*, 50.

Stacte

There has also been controversy over the identification of the incense translated stacte in numerous verses, which is notable because the formula for producing this incense was recorded as long ago as Pliny.[8] Stacte is a fragrance derived from myrrh resin by dissolving the resin in an oil. Myrrh resin does not have an odor. However, the fresh-flowing resin either from incisions or naturally is reported to be redolent.[9] I have not experienced it. Littman et al. provides a summary of stacte and other perfumes and illustrated their preparation, a kind of hands-on cookbook for the compounds.[10]

Like stacte, bdellium is a myrrh product. It is produced from myrrh species in Africa and India and is considered inferior to Arabian myrrh.[11]

---

8. Ben-Yehoshua et al., *Ancient Spices*, 41. This is a helpful review of incense including a welcome discussion of current research.

9. Lucas, *Notes on Myrrh*. Lucas suggests that stacte can either be the freshly exuded sap or the preparation made by dissolving the hardened myrrh in oil or the resin can be pressed to extract the liquid myrrh. Thus, there are three products known in antiquity as liquid myrrh or stacte.

10. Littman et al., *Mendesian Perfumes*.

11. Miller, *Spice Trade*, 69–71, 101–2.

Figure 1. Myrrh east of Salahah, below Jebel Samhan, Oman.

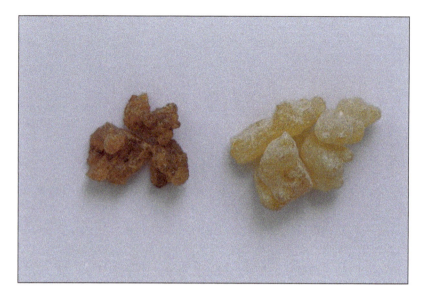

Figure 2. Myrrh resin left, frankincense resin right.

Figure 3. Fresh myrrh resin. This is desirable for preparing stacte. See text. Dhofar, southern Oman.

Figure 4. Shop in northern Ethiopia selling myrrh (dark center sack) and frankincense (sacks above and below myrrh).

MYRTLE

Myrtle was once a popular name. Not until I saw this shrub in its natural habitat did I appreciate why girls were named after this beautiful plant. Because the myrtle is comely and easily cultivated it is widely planted as an ornamental shrub.

Myrtle[1] is an appealing shrub with evergreen leaves. Under optimum conditions it grows to a height of about 8 meters (24 feet). Fragrant, small, white flowers are produced in the middle of the summer. The fruit is a small, black berry, resembling a blueberry, and is edible but with little comestible value.[2] The entire plant contains a fragrant oil which is intensified when the leaves are dry. Like the date palm, the myrtle is the sole representative of its family in the Middle East. The eucalyptus, native to Australia and widely planted in the Middle East, is in the same family.

This plant is not mentioned in the Bible until the time of the captivity. The first reference is in Nehemiah 8:15 in the celebration of the Feast of Tabernacles: "and that they should proclaim this word and spread it throughout their towns and in Jerusalem: 'Go out into the hill country and bring back branches from olive and wild olive trees, and from myrtles, palms, and shade trees, to make temporary shelters'" (NIV). Interestingly, myrtle is not expressly mentioned in Leviticus 23:3–40, which governs the Feast of Tabernacles.

The references in Isaiah (41:19 and 55:13) refer to the establishment of the people in the land. As an evergreen, fragrant shrub associated with watercourses, the myrtle is a fitting symbol of the recovery and establishment of God's promises.

Zechariah 1:8–11 pictures a man standing in a ravine among myrtle trees apparently enjoying their humble beauty and fragrance, appropriate as a ravine or other watercourse is the habitat of the myrtle.

---

1. *Myrtus communis*.

2. In a village in northern Syria near the Turkish border I was served a liqueur made with myrtle fruits. Very tasty! I have also been told that myrtle leaves are added to the still when making the popular Arab liqueur, *aarak*.

However, he does not indicate how these products of myrtle were used. Except for the Feast of Booths, no uses for myrtle are mentioned in the Bible.[3] Other religions also use myrtle for cultic purposes.[4]

Figure 1. Myrtle is an attractive shrub and a common garden subject in suitable climates. Chios, Greece.

---

3. In my ethnobotanical surveys, I found that myrtle branches were used in funeral preparations by Shiite Muslims in Lebanon and that the leaves were used in shampoo for perfuming women's hair in Oman.

4. Dafni et al., *Ritual Plants*, 335.

Figure 2. I purchased these branches of fresh myrtle in the market in Aleppo, Syria from a shop that sells them for use in funerals and burials.

Figure 3. Myrtle branches drying on a ledge of Jebel Akhdar in northern Oman. Puzzled, I asked my Arab colleague who told me the dried leaves were used to scent homemade shampoo. He said the smell reminded him of his grandmother who used it.

NETTLE

Unlike many Bible plants, the nettle is common in both Europe and the Middle East. Some translations use the word nettle for the Hebrew *chārûl* in Job 30:7, Hosea 9:6, and Zephaniah 2:9 and for *qimmôś* in Proverbs 24:30–31.

The most widespread nettle in the Middle East is Roman nettle.[1] The seeds are edible but small and a pain to harvest! Like other nettles, these are weeds that grow in areas of high nitrogen concentration so are most abundant in places where cattle are kept and about human habitations. The entire plant is covered with long, highly specialized hairs that can puncture the skin. Each hair acts as a miniature hypodermic needle. At the tip is a lopsided bulb-like structure that is easily broken at a pre-stressed region. With the slightest touch, the tip falls off leaving the sharp point, which can then easily penetrate the skin. At the base of the hair is a reservoir of irritant, believed to be chemically similar to that injected in ant stings, which is under pressure and escapes through the tip into the victim. The result is a minor dermatitis that will go away in most individuals after thirty minutes or so. This response, known as urticaria, gives the genus its Latin name, *Urtica.*

Though little appreciated today, nettles were valued by ancient cultures as a source of food and fiber.[2] It is not surprising, therefore, that native nettles would be mentioned in the Bible. However, caution is needed as the words translated nettle could mean a different armed plant or, very likely, be a general term for undesirable plants.

---

1. *Urtica pilulifera* Pilulifera refers to the ball-shaped fruits in this species.
2. Grauso et al., *Stinging Nettle*, 1343.

Figure 1. Flowering common nettle along a sidewalk in Amsterdam.

Figure 2. Roman nettle, Kartak, Kurdish Iraq. The distinctive fruits are globose.

OAK

Few Bible trees would be more familiar to the American or European visitor to the Eastern Mediterranean than oaks. Perhaps this familiarity explains the fact that several large trees mentioned in the Bible, such as the Atlantic pistacia, were translated as oaks by Europeans unacquainted with the trees of the Middle East. While Eastern North America has a dozen or more oak species, only a few occur in the Middle East. There has been confusion between translation of the word for pistacias (terebinths) and oaks. (See Pistacia.)

Two of the most common oaks are the Palestine oak[1] and Mt. Tabor oak,[2] though the two are not distinguished from one another in the Bible. Both can become large, long-lived trees with spreading branches. Because of extensive over-grazing and cutting, large oaks are uncommon today. With their size, longevity, and beauty, it is not difficult to see how oaks are objects of veneration, a practice carried out today by some people in the region.

In addition to the two species of oaks mentioned, cedar of Lebanon and Atlantic pistacia would be the biggest trees. All three can be a symbol of a mighty man (e.g., Amos 2:9). In general, the prominent feature of the cedar is its size while that of the oak (and pistacia) is its strength.

Oaks were used for purposes other than timber, including food and tanning. Food is not something we regularly associate with oaks, yet the acorns are nutritious and in some parts of the world were an important source of nutrition.

In addition, oaks were one of the sources of tannin necessary for tanning hides. Another source of tannin are galls on species of oaks and pistacias. While tanning was common in those days, only one incident is mentioned, Simon the tanner in Acts 10:6.

The Bible locates Simon's house (and assumed location of his tannery) near the sea, perhaps for two reasons. First is the necessity for water in the process, which produces a powerful, persistent stench, which could be the second reason for the location.[3] Especially important in the ancient process was the use of oak gall "apples," which are formed when a tiny wasp lays eggs

---

1. *Quercus calliprinos* synonymous with *Q. coccifera*.
2. *Quercus ithaburensis*. Also known as Valonia oak and other common names.
3. Poole and Reed, *Preparation of Leather*, 8, 10, 12, 14.

in the oak. This alters the chemistry of the oak to produce more tannins. Gall apples were ground and used in tanning, a process that helps preserve the leather and make it supple. Gall apples were also used to make ink and various medicines.

Only a fraction of the original oak forests remain due to cutting, overgrazing, and perhaps the greatest insult—wood for Ottoman locomotives to maintain the essential Hejaz Railway at the time of the First World War, which decimated the oaks of Bashan in southeastern Syria.

At one time, the Hauran, including Bashan, was famous for its oaks, the oaks of Bashan are mentioned in the Bible (Zechariah 11:2; Ezekiel 27:6). In the early eleventh century, an Arab traveler by name of Mukaddasi visited the Hauran and writes that the natives subsisted on acorns which they ground and mixed with "desert barley"[4] (which I take to be wild barley).[5] This clearly indicates that oaks were once abundant in the Hauran; only remnants remain.

Lastly, oak makes excellent charcoal. Even though the forest preserves in Jordan prohibit cutting and burning of trees, I have seen "charcoal poaching" at the Zubia Preserve in Jordan.

Figure 1. Mount Tabor oak[6] in Galilee, Israel.

4. *Hordeum spontaneum*, a native barley ancestral to cultivated species.

5. Mukaddasi, *Description of Syria*, 91. "These people feed themselves with acorns—a fruit that is the size of a date, but bitter. They split it in half and make it sweeter by allowing it to soak in water. It is then dried and ground in a mill. In this country also grows desert-barley, which these people mix with the acorn-meal, and therewith make their bread." This description of the preparation of acorns for food is remarkably similar to the practices of other peoples dependent on oaks for food, e.g., Native American nations.

6. *Quercus ithaburensis*.

Figure 2. Aleppo pine, kermes oak[7] forest, Dibeen, Jordan.

Figure 3. Oaks, likely Aleppo oak,[8] in a cemetery in eastern Kurdish Iraq. The rags tied to the tree at the left are left in memory of a person. This practice is widespread in Western Asia as well as in Native American cultures.

7. *Quercus coccifera.*
8. *Quercus infectoria.*

Figure 4. Aleppo oak with many galls caused by wasps. Near Irbil, Kurdish Iraq.

Figure 5. Galls (above) and acorns in a pharmacy in Sulaimani, Kurdish Iraq.

OLIVE

Venerable, utilitarian, and an integral part of Middle Eastern culture, olive use today parallels that of ancient times. In other words, the olive plays a similar role in today's rural society as it did in the days when the Bible were written.

The olive tree is native to the Mediterranean region, but most of its relatives are currently found in Africa.[1]

There are about twenty-five biblical references to the olive tree and more than 160 references to the oil. This oil had five main uses in Bible days: as food, for illumination, as ointment, manufacture of soap, and as leather and metal preservative. It is safe to assume that when oil is mentioned in the Scriptures, it is olive oil. Interestingly, we have no record in the Scriptures of olives themselves being eaten, although the absence of such data does not mean they were not a food item. On the other hand, the Qu'ran records olives as a condiment. "And a tree that grows out of Mount Sinai which produces oil and a condiment for those who eat" (Sura 23:20 Dawood).

The concept of a holy olive tree that provides illumination to God's servants is included in both holy books. In Zechariah 4, the prophet is told that the two oil-producing trees in his vision are two leaders anointed of the Lord (Zerubbabel and Joshua the high priest). These trees provide the oil for the seven-branched golden lampstand he sees beside them. Similarly, in the Qu'ran Sura 24:35 we read of a blessed olive tree that produces an oil that gives light to mankind. Both of these references clearly show the role that olive oil had in illumination in ancient times.

It was, therefore, a daily commodity for the people of the books, an importance reflected in several verses. Disobedience to God would result in a loss of the olive crop (Deuteronomy 28:40). The oil honored both God and men (Judges 9:9) and was a component of the anointing oil of the high priest (Exodus 30:24). Large supplies of oil were a sign of prosperity. The excess oil can be stored for up to six years; such stores were of national concern. For example, in the days of King David, Joash was given the important charge of oil supplies (1 Chronicles 27:28). In addition to lamps, the oil was used as an ointment for the skin (Psalm 104:15), important in

1. Kaniewski et al., *Primary Domestication.*

an arid land. Lesser-known uses are soap (Jeremiah 2:22; Malachi 3:2) and a preservative for shields, perhaps constructed of wood and overlain with leather (2 Samuel 1:21).

The olive tree is one of the most familiar and characteristic trees in the entire region. The oil is especially prized by Arabs, who use it daily. A simple breakfast is just bread and olive oil, often dipped first into a spicy mixture of herbs and salt.

These most venerable of trees are attractive, as indicated in Hosea 14:6 and Psalm 128:3. In the dry season the tree with its dark green leaves contrasts with the dry, brown hills. Leaves are evergreen, dark gray-green above and gray beneath. With a slight breeze, the trees will appear silverish and in the dry season the wind makes the hillsides glisten. This shimmering is due to layers of shield-shaped scales that imbricate the undersurface of the leaf, a mechanism to reduce evaporation of water

Large areas are planted in olives; these thrive on the steep and rocky slopes (see Deuteronomy 32:13) in carefully maintained terraces. The remarkable root system of the olive tree is the secret of its survival in its dry, rocky, habitat. To produce a good crop, however, the trees need attention throughout the year—careful pruning, cultivating, and fertilizing. One of the characteristics of the olive tree is the production of sprouts at its base. Olives are often grown on grafted stock, that is, a rapidly growing rootstock is selected, and a good quality scion is put in it. The olive farmer selects sprouts from his best trees, removes them, and plants them, where they are carefully tended. Psalm 128:3 may be a reference to this practice—"your sons will be like olive shoots round your table" (NIV).[2]

The olive tree does not become very tall and lives for up to one thousand years producing fruit season after season. Trunks often become gnarled, bent, and hollow inside, yet the tree continues to produce fruit. Because of this growth pattern, the wood is unsuitable for building but is hard with an attractive grain and is used today for the manufacture of small souvenirs.

Olive wood is mentioned only in 1 Kings 6 for the construction of the doors in the temple. It would be difficult to find a piece of olive wood large enough to make a door. It has been suggested that this could be sandalwood, not native to Israel, but imported from India. Possibly the doors were made from a composite of many small pieces of olive wood fastened together. The identity of this wood remains unknown.

---

2. Steinmann, *Arboreal Imagery*, 3. Steinmann's application would be stronger if he was aware (?) of the sprouts produced by olives.

About May 1st, the olive begins to flower. The flowers are only slightly scented, white, and small, often hidden in the branches. Though attractive, they are humble kin compared to other showy fragrant members of the same family, flowering shrubs like lilac, forsythia, and jasmine. Olives are more utilitarian, valued for their fruit.

In the autumn, olives begin to produce their fruit. They are harvested as in Bible times by carefully beating the trees with sticks and then picking up the green olives from the ground, often from sheets that have been spread beneath the tree.

When ripe, the olive is jet black and attractive. If you enjoy olives, you would be tempted to eat one right off the tree. Looks are deceiving! The fresh olive is very bitter and unpalatable and must be crushed to express the oil and separate it from the bitter aqueous component. Until recently, olives were crushed in villages between giant stones driven by draft animals. Today hydraulic presses are used. In order to be palatable, the green olives must be soaked in a brine to remove the bitter component in the aqueous part of the fruit. Cracking the olive speeds up this process.

What is the wild olive tree mentioned in Nehemiah 8:15 and Romans 11:17? The Nehemiah reference is likely not a wild olive (see Pine) but the only New Testament reference in Romans undoubtedly notes a wild or at least uncultivated olive. Farmers have referred to trees that spontaneously come up in their olive groves as wild olives. These have a much different aspect than the carefully cultivated trees, but they probably only represent an offshoot from the larger population.

Olive oil was needed for soap production. Today, there is still an industry for soap production from olive oil. Arab friends insist it is the best soap because so much effort is needed to produce a lather. A helpful review of soap production, past and present, is found in Arbel.[3]

---

3. Arbel, *Olive Oil Soap*.

Figure 1. Olive trees often obtain grotesque growth forms as they age, such as this tree in Monopoli, Italy.

Figure 2. Harvesting olives in Kufur Sumei, Galilee, Israel.

Figure 3. The Mount of Olives is the ridge at the top of the image where there are numerous old olive trees, but none known to go back to the days of Jesus, despite what the tourist guide says.

Figure 4. Olive trees sprout from the base, a horticultural feature noted in the Scriptures. Sidi Bou Ghaba, Morocco.

Figure 5. The four-parted flowers of olive are fragrant, but usually not apparent with the evergreen dense foliage. Antakya (ancient Antioch), Turkey.

Figure 6. The wood of olive is not suitable for timber in construction because of the numerous fissures, but is valued for making artifacts like these bowels purchased in Bethlehem.

ONION

Despite the fact that onion[1] is an essential component of Middle East cuisine, there is only a solitary reference to it in the Bible. This is another example of how the abundance of a vegetable or other plant is not proportional to its inclusion in the sacred writings. Other examples of this scant representation include lentils and beans.

But onions were obviously appreciated and eagerly sought after as attested by the laments from the children of Israel, who bemoaned the lack of onions in the wilderness (Numbers 11:5). The origins of the cultivated onion are still being debated.[2] What is certain is that it is an ancient food.

In fact, onion has been a food for millennia, both in Egypt and Mesopotamia.[3] Onion is easily grown from seed and after germination the small seedlings are set out to mature. While the main use of onion was obviously as a food, onions have been found inside mummies, indicating a role in the preservation of the body or as an aid to the person in the afterlife.

1. *Allium cepa.*
2. Zohary, *Domestication*, 157.
3. Murray, *Egypt Condiments*, 628–30.

ONION 219

Figure 1. Field of flowering onion near Zababdeh, Palestinian Territory.

Figure 2. Watchtower in onion field south of Ramallah, Palestinian Territory. Note the weeds in the field. As in ancient times, this field has not been weeded.

PAPYRUS

The identity of the few wetland plants mentioned in the Bible have been subject to some confusion. For example, in the most recent treatment of this group, various plants, including rushes, reeds, and papyrus, are lumped together. I believe, however, that a finer resolution is possible using the settings of the texts. The papyrus plant is mentioned in Exodus 23:3 (along the Nile), Job 8:11 (which notes the tall habit of the plant), Job 9:26 and Isaiah 18:2 (both referring to boats constructed of papyrus), and Isaiah 35:7 (which accurately describes the ecology of papyrus). Papyrus[1] best fits the verses noted above. (For the places where the Hebrew word *gome'* is used [Job 8:11; Isaiah 35:7], see Reed.)

Papyrus is a chiefly tropical plant, widespread in Africa with only a few outliers in the Middle East. Once abundant in the Nile Delta, it was virtually extirpated by the time of Napoleon's invasion of Egypt. The only extant population in the Middle East is in the Hula Swamp in northern Israel, where considerable efforts at protection and restoration of the papyrus-dominated swamp have been undertaken.

These are impressive aquatic plants reaching as tall as 10 feet (3.5 meters) with large globe-shaped masses of flowers. The stems are tough and spongy and were traditionally used for the construction of skiffs as well as mats, baskets, and other items.

In the account of the construction of the protective ark for baby Moses in Exodus 2, the logical plant is papyrus because of its abundance in the Nile region. Likewise, in Isaiah 18:2b, speaking of Cush, modern Ethiopia: "Woe to the land of whirring wings along the rivers of Cush, which sends envoys by sea in papyrus boats over the water" (NIV). The choice of papyrus for *gome'* seems best because the other possibilities, reed and cane, were not used to make boats.

The only mention of paper in the Bible is 2 John 12a: "Having many things to write unto you, I would not write with paper and ink" (ESV). By the time of the New Testament paper was being used in addition to parchment. In the Levant paper was made chiefly from papyrus.

---

1. *Cyperus papyrus.*

Figure 1. Papyrus marsh along the edge of the Okavango River, northern Namibia.

Figure 2. Flowering and fruiting heads of papyrus.

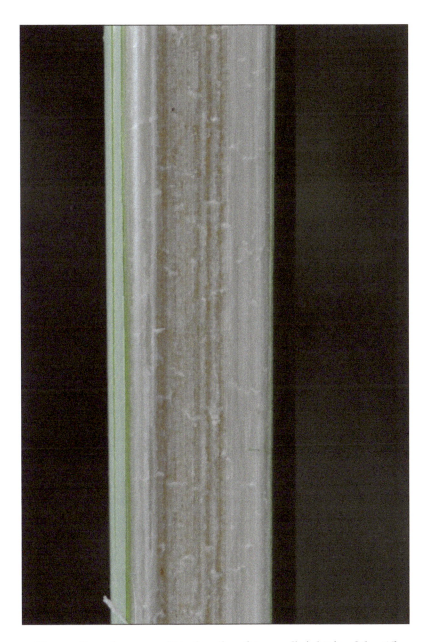

Figure 3. Stem of papyrus split to show the soft inner cells (white) and the stiff green outer cells. Stems like these when pounded together make paper.

PINE

Everyone knows the general architecture of a pine tree, that they have cones, and that the sap of the tree is resinous and sticky. Because of this knowledge, European translators may have erroneously translated as pine the trees they encountered in the texts. The ancients based their plant taxonomy on the *uses* of plants as well as similar morphology. Of course, neither morphology nor uses indicate the evolution of the plant. This is especially true for coniferous trees, where it is not clear if fir, pine, cypress, or junipers are intended.

The Cilician fir,[1] a valued timber tree, is protected in Syria and Lebanon. It is not certain that there were more extensive stands in Bible days. In fact, historically the trees in the Levant have been considered relictual.[2] Pines, on other hand, even today have considerable stands.

Three pines are frequently found in the Middle East. One, the stone pine[3] (because of its hard seeds), also known as umbrella pine (in allusion to its umbrella-like appearance when mature), is grown for its seeds which are an important ingredient in Middle East foods and one of the ten most important nut trees in the world.[4] Today, most of these seeds are imported from China and may be produced by trees other than the stone pine. And there is evidence that cultivation of stone pine, a Mediterranean species native to parts of northern Lebanon and Syria, was not widespread in ancient times.[5]

These same authors suggest that Calabrian pine[6] (common name after the Calabria region of Italy) did not occur in ancient Israel.[7]

There are remnant forests of Aleppo pine[8] in Israel and Jordan.[9] Calabrian pine is present in Syria and widespread in Turkey. While it is the

1. *Abies cilicia.*
2. Alizoti et al., *Mediterranean Firs*, 4.
3. *Pinus pinaea.* Also known as Italian stone pine.
4. Fady et al., *Stone Pine.*
5. Liphschitz et al., *Masada Timber.*
6. *Pinus brutia.* Also known as brutia pine as a common name.
7. Bigger and Liphschitz, *Calabrian Pine.*
8. *Pinus halepensis.*
9. Fady et al., *Aleppo and Brutia Pines.*

most abundant pine in the Levant, there is convincing evidence that Aleppo pine was never widespread in what is modern day Israel and Jordan.

Aleppo and Calabrian pine are quite similar, and I have difficulty readily distinguishing them in the field. Despite their similarity, there is reproductive and genetic evidence that they represent two distinct species. In common with many pines, both the Aleppo and Calabrian pines belong to fire-maintained plant communities.

Among adaptations to fire are persistent lower branches that can carry flame to the crowns of the trees where the cones will open in response to heat. Both of these pines have serotinous cones, that is, retention of mature seeds in a canopy-stored seed bank that ensures delayed dispersal in response to fire. In general, pines that have non-pruning branches do not produce the most desirable timber because of the presence of knots that weaken the ability of the wood to carry weight. Therefore, it is unlikely that pine was used in the same way as, for example, cedar or open grown (in contrast to fastigate) cypress which have long boles (the distance from the ground to the first branch).

In light of these considerations, is pine mentioned anywhere in the Bible? I don't think it is possible to say with certainty that any verses explicitly refer to pine. But there is a pine product that is often overlooked when considering trees in the Bible.

That product is naval stores (an archaic English term linked with the role of these products in sailing ships): pitch, tar, and resin—materials extracted from pine trees for caulking ships and sealing wine amphora. Both Aleppo and Calabrian are recorded as producing pitch and turpentine in the ancient Mediterranean.[10] It could be that the pitch in Noah's ark (Genesis 6:14) was derived from pine. Perhaps the pitch in Moses' basket (Exodus 2:3) was also from pine, or from bitumen. Pine resin was also used to seal amphorae containing wine, especially in regions where the more desirable resin/gum of terebinth was not available.[11] Resin from pines and other gymnosperms were used in the Assyrian Empire for the production of soap.[12]

Whether or not pine can be documented as being in the Bible, it is an important and conspicuous element of the landscape in areas of the Levant with higher rainfall. Like many pines, those occurring in the lands we are considering are adapted to frequent fires in their habitats.

---

10. Meiggs, *Trees and Timber*, 466–71.

11. Mills and White, *Identity of Resins*, 37.

12. Levey, *Pine Soap*. The use of pine resin in the production soap was widespread in Colonial America.

Figure 1. Umbrella pines in background which are the source of the drying cones on the roof of my colleague's house in the Chouf region of Mount Lebanon. The trees exhibit the characteristic umbrella-shaped crown.

Figure 2. Seeds of the umbrella pine. The seeds have to be further processed to extricate the edible seed from the hard shell.

Figure 3. Calabrian pine with cones adapted to opening by fire. Mount Lebanon.

Figure 4. The most common pine in the Levant is the Aleppo pine, which has distinctively stalked cones. Mount Gerazim, Palestinian Territory.

PISTACHIO

Native to the Near East and Southwest Asia the pistachio tree[1] has been widely cultivated in the Middle East for millennia[2] so it is not unusual that Jacob would include them as a special treat from Canaan to present to the leader of Egypt (Genesis 37:25). The region of Aleppo, Syria is famous for its pistachios and in that area they are known in Arabic as "nuts of Aleppo." Turkey, Iran, and the United States are today's largest producers.

Poison ivy is in the same family as pistachio as well as mangos and cashews and persons with a strong reaction to poison ivy and evil ilk poison oak and poison sumac should avoid raw pistachios (as well as raw cashews and unripe mangos). Like its toxic relatives, the flowers of pistachio are green and inconspicuous. Pistachio trees have a broad crown and dark green, compound leaves. Each tree is unisexual so a grove of trees must include some male as well as predominantly female plants. There are two other species of the same genus in the Middle East Atlantic terebinth, and Palestine terebinth. Like these relatives, the fruit of the pistachio is covered with a leathery red covering. This is the reason pistachios are often dyed bright red before being sold.

1. *Pistacia vera.*
2. Rousou et al., *Archaeobotanical Pistacia.*

Figure 1. A fruiting branch in a pistachio orchard south of Aleppo.

Figure 2. Fresh raw pistachios with the fleshy fruit coat intact purchased from a street vendor in Amman, Jordan. These contain small amounts of the irritant in poison ivy and should be avoided by those with a strong reaction to poison ivy. The taste is resinous and inferior, in my opinion to the roasted nuts.

PLANE TREE

The plane tree[1] can live to a great age and attain a very large circumference. As a result, it often has immense boughs, as intimated in Ezekiel 31:8 "The cedars in the garden of God could not rival it, nor the fir trees equal its boughs; neither were the plane trees like its branches; no tree in the garden of God was its equal in beauty" (v. 8 ESV). This description, comparing Pharaoh to trees, draws upon the image of a well-known tree found in moist soil in the Middle East, often along streams. The Geneva Bible and King James translate this as chestnut, a tree not native to the Levant.

Genesis 30 describes Jacob's attempt at genetic engineering. He placed peeled branches of trees in front of mating cattle to influence the color of their offspring. One of these branches was from the plane tree (Genesis 30:37). The bark of the mature plane tree is mottled with brown patches of rough bark against smooth, white bark and bears a resemblance to the markings on the cattle. Only the young branches are white, but the inner bark would appear whitish when peeled, features of the other woody plants that Jacob used.

This species is a desirable garden subject because of its growth form, ease of cultivation, and attractive bark, which is often white. Its value as an ornamental is testified by the inclusion of the plane tree in the courtyard garden of Herod the Great.[2]

The plane tree is widespread throughout Western Asia, native to watercourses and other wet places, but also widely planted because it is easy to grow and attains a large size, affording ample shade. It would be familiar to residents of the region and a suitable image for strength and majesty.

---

1. *Platanus orientalis*. The common and similar in appearance sycamore of eastern North America is *P. occidentalis*.
2. Langgut and Gleason, *Garden of King Herod*, 89.

Figure 1. The young trunks and branches of the plane tree are often white, as here, and with age develop brown splotches. Platres, Cyprus.

PLANE TREE 233

Figure 2. Mottled bark of the plane tree. Dimet, Chouf Region, Mount Lebanon.

POMEGRANATE

Pomegranate, one of the six species of the land (Deuteronomy 8:8), is perhaps the most appealing of all six, with beautiful flowers and attractive fruits. It is an easily cultivated shrub bearing crimson red to orange flowers in the spring and summer from which the large, grapefruit-sized fruits develop in the late summer and autumn.

The fruits are unusual in containing seeds that have a highly specialized seed coat that is fleshy rather than hard. This fleshy layer is the source of the juice for which the pomegranate is prized. There are innumerable cultivars, including some with yellow fruits. In general, however, they can be divided into two main categories—those with sweet and those with sour juice. The seeds are also eaten in some countries. The leathery covering of the fruit allows it to be stored for a long time, and a dye can be prepared from the rind.

It is the beauty of the pomegranate, rather than its culinary use, that is most frequent in the Bible. The border of the skirt of the high priest was ornamented with pomegranates (Exodus 28:33–34; 39:24) as were the pillars in Solomon's temple (1 Kings 7:18, 20; 2 Kings 25:17; 2 Chronicles 3:16; 4:13; Jeremiah 52:22).

The Song of Solomon contains numerous references to the beauty of the pomegranate, emphasizing the red color: "Your cheeks are like rosy pomegranates behind your veil" (Song of Solomon 4:3 NLT). Also in Song of Solomon 6:7.

The reference later in that chapter (4:13) has been variously translated, in the ASV: "Thy shoots are an orchard of pomegranates, with precious fruits; henna with spikenard plants" while in the NLT: "Your thighs shelter a paradise of pomegranates with rare spices—henna with nard," perhaps best capturing the erotic tone of the book.

Flowers are referred to in 6:11: "I went down to the orchard of nut trees to see the blossoms of the valley, to see whether the vine had budded or the pomegranates had bloomed" (NASB).

Pomegranate juice is mentioned only in Song of Solomon 8:2. This ancient beverage is now available in most American supermarkets, touted for its health benefits, for which there is ample evidence from recent studies.

The two references in the minor prophets (Joel 1:12; Haggai 2:19) refer to the demise of pomegranate along with other crops as a sign of divine judgment. Pomegranate is not mentioned in the New Testament.

Figure 1. Pomegranate flowering branch. Efes, Turkey.

Figure 2. Ripening fruits, Cana, Galilee. The seeds of pomegranate are distinct in having a fleshy seed coat, which is the source of the juice. The wall of the fruit, the rind, is rich in tannins and has been used as a medicine.

POPLARS

Poplars are fast-growing trees with soft wood and often favor wet areas. The seeds have long, silky hairs that aid in dispersal. A mass of these resembles cotton, hence the common name of cottonwood in English for many of these trees.

Euphrates Poplar

The helpful treatment by Royle[1] has unfortunately not received due attention for clarifying a word (Hebrew *bākhā'*) that has been variously translated.[2] Like most, the King James translation of Psalm 84:6 leaves the word untranslated ("Who passing through the valley of Baca make it a well; the rain also filleth the pools"). The incident in the story of Absalom's rebellion which includes this word has been translated as mulberry[3] (KJV) or balsam (ESV, NASB, NIV, NJB) while the NLT is more botanically accurate: "But after a while the Philistines returned and raided the valley again. And once again David asked God what to do. 'Do not attack them straight on' God replied. 'Instead, circle around behind and attack them near the poplar trees. When you hear a sound like marching feet in the tops of the poplar trees, go out and attack! That will be the signal that God is moving ahead of you to strike down the Philistine army'" (2 Samuel 5:23–24). This story is repeated in 1 Chronicles 14:14.

As Royle notes, the tree in these verses should favor wet sites (valleys, near pools) and have leaves easily rustled, both features of poplars. The petiole (leaf stalk) of Euphrates poplar, like other poplar species, has an aerodynamic foil that greatly amplify the very slightest breeze, causing the

---

1. Royle was a well-respected botany professor at King's College and also held several positions in India. Like George Edward Post, Royle may be one of those few experts in botany and the Bible.

2. Royle, *Biblical Literature Baca*, 276–77.

3. Coles, *Mulberry*, 86–88. Coles points out that the presence of mulberry in Israel at the time of Absalom's rebellion is debatable. The curt description of the habitat in the Bible also militates against the trees being mulberries.

leaves to tremble even when the air appears virtually motionless. Hence the name trembling aspen[4] for one of the most widespread trees of the northern United States and Canada. An additional feature of poplar leaves is their stiff nature providing more noise when rustled than less stiff leaves.

One of the most frequent trees of riverine habitats in the Middle East is the Euphrates poplar,[5] common in the Jordan Valley and along the Euphrates and Tigris Rivers. It best meets the criteria suggested by this verse—wet habitat, easily rustled, and stiff leaves that would make a louder noise than many other trees. Isaiah 44:4 also gives clear indication of the ecology of this poplar: "They will spring up like grass in a meadow, like poplar trees by flowing streams" (NIV).

Like other poplars, Euphrates poplar is a rapidly growing tree with soft wood, unsuitable for most uses except crude lumber and withes. It could be the tree mentioned in Jeremiah 12:5 as the "thickets of the Jordan" (NLT) or that could be the related willow (species of the genus *Salix*, which is in the same family as the poplar, the Salicaceae. See Willow).

In the verses noted above, I believe *bākhā'* is best translated as Euphrates poplar. Leviticus 23:40 suggests trees with ample leaves, a feature more characteristic of poplar than willow. The well-known verse in Psalm 137:2 where the children of Israel hang their harps on the "willows" of Babylon could be either the Euphrates poplar or a true willow, both are abundant along the Euphrates.

White Poplar

White poplar,[6] with white bark and white leaf undersurface, is native to the Middle East and may be the tree in Genesis 30:37. "Jacob, however, took fresh-cut branches from poplar, almond and plane trees and made white stripes on them by peeling the bark and exposing the white inner wood of the branches" (NIV). White poplar, also known as silver poplar, favors wet areas. For this reason, I question whether the tree translated poplar for mountaintop sacrificial site could be white poplar.

---

4. *Populus tremuloides*.
5. *Populus euphratica*.
6. *Populus alba*.

Figure 1. Along a branch of the Tigris River in eastern Iraq in June. This tree has varying leaf shapes on a single shrub.

Figure 2. The leaf stalk of Euphrates poplar showing the knife-like edge which catches the slightest air current, causing the leaves to rustle (2 Samuel 5:24).

Figure 3. Euphrates poplar with its characteristic blue-green leaves is in the center with willows on either side. Along the Chami Razan River in eastern Iraq.

Figure 4. Flowering Euphrates poplar long the Euphrates River, Deir Ezzor, Syria.

Figure 5. Euphrates poplar in fruit. The small seeds have long hairs to aid in wind dispersal, like other poplars given the name cottonwood for that reason.
Chami Razan, Kurdish Iraq

Figure 6. White poplar along a stream in the Atlas Mountains, Morocco.

Figure 7. The densely hairy undersurface of a white poplar leaf.

REED

Common reed,[1] *like cane,* is also a member of the grass family though characteristically found in wetter sites than cane. It is one of the few plants that grows throughout most of the world. Large stands are found in the delta of the Danube near the Black Sea. In North America, the same species has developed especially aggressive races that are destroying some natural wetlands. Common reed is frequent throughout the Middle East. Reaching a height of 4 meters (12 feet), it is a hardy plant of marshes with tough, aggressive rhizomes.

Jeremiah 51:31–32 is a graphic description of battles in Babylon, a city located along rivers with marshes. "One courier follows another and messenger follows messenger to announce to the king of Babylon that his entire city is captured, the river crossings seized, the marshes set on fire and the soldiers terrified" (NIV). The reeds here are ablaze. Babylon's marshes may have been dominated by common reed, which forms dense stands along the Tigris and Euphrates as well as in oases.

One such oasis is the famed Azraq Oasis in Jordan, which has suffered from reckless draining in recent years. Further damage has been incurred by the removal of water for the city of Amman. The permanent lakes at Azraq made it the largest oasis in hundreds of square kilometers of desert. With a lowering of the water table, common reed invaded and today forms the dominant vegetation in the vastly reduced oasis, which, ironically, must be maintained by pumping water into it.

March 19th was a bright, still day when I visited Azraq Oasis with other biologists. Concerned about the overwhelming dominance of reed that crowded out other more desirable species and lowered diversity of plants and animals, we surveyed the area and then left for the Azraq Preserve office on a low hill overlooking the marsh. Suddenly the sky was filled with billows of black smoke from the marsh. The stand of common reed was ablaze. Rushing to the fire we were rebuffed by the roar and heat. As the reed burns, water vapor builds up in the stem causing a popping sound. I could identify with the soldiers at the margin of the marsh in Jeremiah 51 terrified as the marsh burns out of control!

1. *Phragmites australis.*

Although not explicated in the Bible reed had several uses in the Middle East.[2] Like cane, the stems could be used to make writing quills. And the leaves and stems were used to weave mats, some of which have survived in Egyptian tombs.[3]

Figure 1. Reed in a seep at Wadi Tarabat, El Ein, United Arab Emirates.

2. Köbbing et al., *Reed Review*.
3. Wendrich, *Reed Basketry*.

Figure 2. Euphrates River near Raqaa, Syria. The pile of reed is drying to be used as fuel.

Figure 3. Mud and waddle building constructed with reeds in the roof. Tel Tamir, Syria

Figure 4. Jordan River lined on both sides by reeds. Near the Baptismal Site, Jordan.

Figure 5. Harvesting reed for construction. Chami Razan, Kurdish Iraq.

RUE

Rue[1] is mentioned only in this verse: "But woe to you Pharisees! For you tithe mint and rue and every herb, and neglect justice and the love of God" (Luke 11:42 ESV) along with "every herb," perhaps an allusion to Deuteronomy 14:22, which required a tithe of all crops.

Rue is a short-lived perennial growing to a height of 3 feet (1 meter) with bright yellow flowers in the late spring. The entire plant is suffused with aromatic oils. The leaves are the part used.

As with the other spices and herbs associated with pharisaical tithing, the scriptures do not tell us how these plant products were used. For this we are dependent upon other sources, including archeological and current indigenous practices.[2] The situation with rue is particularly interesting as it contains several compounds that are toxic in higher doses. In Palestinian villages, I have eaten black olives cured with chopped rue leaves, a practice not to be encouraged considering the considerable literature on its toxicity.

I question whether rue was used as a spice in Bible days, at least not as something that was added to flavor food. It is well documented as the cause of photosensitization, which occurs when a plant compound enters the skin and then is exposed to ultraviolet light, which alters the composition of the compound, causing eruptions.[3]

Considering its documented medical uses since ancient times, I suggest that it may have been grown as a medicine. The writer of Luke was a physician, and it is interesting that it is only mentioned in his gospel.

---

1. *Ruta chalepensis.* There are species other than this Mediterranean native.

2. Andrews, *Use of Rue,* provides a review of traditional uses of rue. Google Scholar gives over 17,000 results for a search "ruta medicine" since 2018 (January 9, 2022).

3. Eickhorst, *Rue the Herb.* This report deals with *Ruta graveolens.*

Figure 1. Fringed rue.[4] The grey-green color of the leaves is characteristic. South of Amman, Jordan.

Figure 2. Strong smelling rue.[5] The bright-yellow flowers yield a capsule with many small seeds. My garden.

4. *Ruta chalepensis.*
5. *Ruta graveolens.*

SAFFRON

"*Your shoots are an* orchard of pomegranates with all choicest fruits, henna with nard, nard and saffron, calamus and cinnamon, with all trees of frankincense, myrrh, and aloes, with all chief spices" (Song of Solomon 4:14 ESV). This is the only place in the Bible where saffron[1] is mentioned. The setting is significant as it is in a garden of fragrant plants, some of which are better known for other purposes today, such as henna as a dye and saffron as a spice. The origin of saffron is not known, but is likely Western Asia.

Like other gustatory topics, spices for foods are seldom mentioned in the Bible. This despite the ancient history of saffron as a spice, medicine, and dye.[2] Because of its increased use in medicine, there is concern today over quality control and adulteration.[3]

Saffron is a true crocus, with grass-like leaves and showy flowers that arise from a bulb (technically a corm) which dies back to the rootstock after flowering. The flowers of saffron are purple with a strong, fragrant aroma. Unlike most other crocus species, saffron does not reproduce sexually and can only be propagated from offshoots of the corm.[4] The spice saffron is derived from the dried stigmata (female pollen receiving structures) and is the costliest spice in the world. The pleasantly bitter taste and bright yellow color are valued culinary attributes.

But in the Bible this use is not mentioned. Rather, it is the fragrant flowers that are noted—a fragrance linked with such products as frankincense, myrrh, spikenard, and aloes (aloeswood).

---

1. *Crocus sativus*.

2. Trakoli, *Saffron Gatherers*. This is a lucid review of the cultural impacts of saffron in ancient Greece.

3. Gohari et al., *Overview of Saffron*. The authors refer to the adulteration of saffron with dried flowers of safflower (*Carthamnus tinctorius*), a common practice in Middle East markets visited by tourists. I have seen safflower flowers for sale in Old Jerusalem ogled by tourists because of the unbelievable low price of "saffron." Palestinian friends use safflower when cooking rice, not for the flavor but for the color.

4. There are native crocus species from which the stigmata ("threads") are collected and used as true saffron by villagers on Mount Lebanon. Caution is needed, however, as some species of crocus and plants that resemble them can be quite toxic.

Figure 1. Saffron flowers in my garden. The red "threads" (stigmata) are part of the female structure and the source of the spice. The leaves are narrow and grass-like with a white stripe on the upper surface.

Figure 2. Saffron "bulbs" (technically corms) dug when the saffron is harvested. Smaller bulbs are discarded, those two years old are replanted for flowers in the next harvest. Ourika, Morocco.

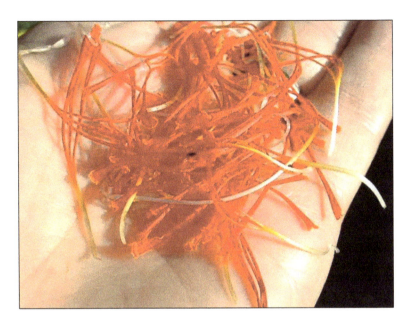

Figure 3. Threads from ten flowers.

Figure 4. Dried flowers of safflower[5] sold in the Old City of Jerusalem. It is often foisted on tourists as saffron and frequently used as an adulterant in saffron.

5. *Carthamus tinctorius.*

SPIKENARD

Though cited only thrice in the Bible, spikenard or nard,[1] is one of the better-known perfumed plants of the Scriptures. It is included in Solomon's Song, in the garden of sensuous delight to which the Lover compares his Beloved: "Your plants are an orchard of pomegranates with choice fruits, with henna and nard, nard and saffron, calamus and cinnamon, with every kind of incense tree, with myrrh and aloes and all the finest spices" (Song of Solomon 4:13–15 NIV).

But the best-known story of nard is in the life of Jesus in John 12: "Then Mary took about a pint of pure nard, an expensive perfume; she poured it on Jesus' feet and wiped his feet with her hair. And the house was filled with the fragrance of the perfume. But one of his disciples, Judas Iscariot, who was later to betray him, objected, 'Why wasn't this perfume sold and the money given to the poor? It was worth a year's wages'" (vv. 3–5 NIV).

The account in John's Gospel indicates the worth of the ointment, which, even considering Semitic hyperbole, was great. Nard was traded extensively in ancient times.[2] The plant and its products are highly valued today, as well, especially in ayurvedic medicine.

Because of demand for the plant in India and other countries, there has been exploitation of this Himalayan species.[3] Nard is rhizomatous and the parts used include the rhizome and sometimes the leaves, which means the plant is destroyed when harvested. The dried rhizome is used for a variety of remedies. An oil can be extracted as well. Collecting pressures have resulted in considerable adulteration of spikenard products further complicated by confusion over common names of the plants, which are known by the general name *jatamansi*. Tangled use of common names as well as proper taxonomy is discussed by Mabberley and Noltie.[4] Conara et al. have surveyed ways to identify adulterants.[5]

1. *Nardostachys jatamansi*.
2. Miller, *Spice Trade*, 88–92.
3. Kaur et al., *Dwindling Resource*.
4. Mabberley and Noltie, *Valeriana Jatamansi*.
5. Cornara et al., *Functional Screening*.

Nard belongs to a group of plants like frankincense, myrrh, and thyine that were widely used in the Middle East, though not cultivated there.

Figure 1. Habitat of spikenard near Lauribinayak, Rasuwa, Nepal.

Figure 2. Indian valerian[6] rhizomes above, spikenard roots/rhizomes below.

6. *Valeriana jatamansi.*

Figure 3. Spikenard just beginning to flower. Lauribinayak, Rasuwa, Nepal

SYCOMORE

Sycomore is a kind of fig and should not be confused with the widespread American sycamore,[1] nor the commonly planted shade tree in Britain that is also called sycamore.[2] It is unfortunate that the English Standard Version uses the spelling sycamore rather than sycomore.[3] Sycamore-fig, as in the New International Version is more descriptive. This fig is native to Africa but was introduced into Egypt in antiquity and was widely planted in ancient Israel, as noted in 1 Kings 10:27, where the allusion to the widespread use of cedar is compared to the common sycomore: "And valuable cedar timber was as common as the sycamore-fig trees that grow in the foothills of Judah" (NLT. See also 2 Chronicles 1:15 and 9:27).

Sycomore can become very large tree. The trunks can reach impressive sizes and so were valued for making coffins and other articles requiring timber of that girth. Thus their destruction would require almost supernatural power, as suggested in Psalm 78:47. Likewise, the large size of the tree is used as an example of faith empowering great feats in Luke 17:6: "And the Lord said, If ye had faith as a grain of mustard seed, ye might say unto this sycamine [sycomore] tree, Be thou plucked up by the root, and be thou planted in the sea; and it should obey you" (KJV). The use of mulberry for the Greek as in ESV, NASB, and NIV is unfortunate and confusing. (See Mulberry.)

Like its relative common fig, sycomore has a highly specialized floral system with tiny, unisexual flowers enclosed in a plum-sized receptacle, the syconium. And like fig, the sycomore produces valued fruits that, however, require special husbandry.

We find reference to the culture of the sycomore in the book of Amos. The prophet tells of his association with this tree: "Then Amos answered and said to [King] Amaziah, 'I was no prophet, nor a prophet's son, but I was a herdsman and a dresser of sycamore figs'" (Amos 7:14 ESV). In order for

1. *Platanus occidentalis.*
2. *Acer pseudoplatanus.*
3. The etymology would require sycomore because the fruit is known by the botanical technical term *syconium* (which incidentally, is the root for sycophant, a word now familiar due to Trumpism). The bark of the sycamore can resemble the bark of the sycomore, hence the confusion in common names.

fruits to develop, they needed to be slightly gashed before maturity; an ancient practice, gashed sycomore figs have been recovered from Egyptian tombs.[4]

In an extensive review of sycomore and the life of the prophet Amos, Steiner points out the connection between being a herdsman and being a keeper of sycomore. The large leaves of the sycomore could be used as fodder, especially during times of drought.[5]

In the well-known story of Zacchaeus, a resident of Jericho climbed into a sycomore in order to see Jesus. The low, spreading branches of a sycomore make it suited for climbing.

Figure 1. Sycomore in Namibia showing the distinctive fruiting branches arising directly from the trunk.

4. Steiner, *Sycomores from Sheba*.
5. Steiner, *Sycomores from Sheba*.

Figure 2. Fruiting sycomore in Ethiopia.

Figure 3. Ripe sycomore figs from Sidon, Lebanon. Note the gashes needed for the maturation of the fruit.

TAMARISK

Just about the only tree that inhabits the shores of the Dead Sea and other hypersaline regions are species of tamarisk.[1] They can do this because, like some other desert shrubs and trees, tamarisks have incredibly long tap roots, capable of extending meters into the desert soil to obtain fresh water.

The genus contains species of trees and shrubs typically found in arid and saline regions. They are common in the Arabian Peninsula and throughout the Middle East. Two species are frequent in the Middle East: athel tamarisk[2] and Nile tamarisk.[3] The number of species as well as species delineation is unclear.[4]

The leaves are tiny, scale-like, and crowded, giving a heath-like appearance. On the leaves are glands that actively secret salt from the soil. During the day the plants secrete salt, at night the salt absorbs water, which evaporates in the morning sun, cooling anyone sleeping under it.

Flowers are small and white or pink, their large masses forming attractive displays. The ripe capsules release seeds with long hairs aiding in wind distribution, one of the reasons several species are invasive. In addition, tamarix is rhizomatous, rapidly spreading, another reason tamarix species have become such pests.

Wood of tamarix is hard and durable. Trunks of tamarisk were used in the fortifications of Masada, no doubt because this is one of the few woody plants of any size in the Dead Sea region.[5]

Two plants are mentioned in Genesis 21. The first is the shrub under which Hagar placed Ishmael (v. 15). The shrub could also easily be a tamarisk as this is one of the most common shrubs and trees in the vicinity of Beersheba. The second is the tamarisk planted by Abraham: "Then Abraham planted a tamarisk tree at Beersheba, and there he worshiped the Lord, the Eternal God" (v. 33 NLT).

1. Species of the genus *Tamarix*.
2. *Tamarix aphylla*.
3. *Tamarix nilotica*.
4. Villar, *Genus Tamarix*.
5. Liphschitz et al., *Masada Timber*.

Why did Abraham plant a tamarisk? Trees were often used as memorials for great men. It is therefore appropriate that Abraham should honor God by planting the tamarisk. It would be a permanent memorial of the covenant between the two.

Saul held court under a tamarisk in Gibeah: "Now Saul heard that David and his men had been discovered. And Saul, spear in hand, was seated under the tamarisk tree on the hill at Gibeah, with all his officials standing around him" (1 Samuel 22:6 NIV). This dark green tree would be obvious from the hilltop and provide a gathering spot, taking advantage of the tree's natural air conditioning as the water evaporated in the morning. However, this was probably a planted tamarisk, as Gibeah is in the Mountains of Judea (now a suburb of Jerusalem) where tamarisks are not native. In 1 Samuel 31:13 Saul is buried under a tamarisk tree while in 1 Chronicles 10:12 the reference is to a pistacia (or terebinth) tree. This apparent discrepancy can be explained by the fact that the word for tamarisk can also be translated as "grove" or perhaps the verse simply means a large tree.

Tamarisk may be visiting an area near you, if you live in the western United States or some other arid region. Several species have been introduced and are becoming aggressive due to their fecundity and ability to grow in waste areas.

Figure 1. Nile tamarisk[6] on shores of the Dead Sea, Jordan.

---

6. Tentative determination.

Figure 2. Athel tamarisk north of Aqaba, Jordan. This could be a planted tree.

Figure 3. French tamarix[7] in flower on shore of Lake Iznik (Nicaea), Turkey.

7. *Tamarix gallica*, tentative determination.

Figure 4. Salt encrusted stem of athel tamarix, Wadi Tarabat, El Ein, United Arab Emirates.

TARES

"*Separating wheat from tares*" is a common expression based on one of the better-known parables of Jesus. But what is tares, mentioned only in Matthew 13? The Greek word *zizania* has been variously translated as tares, darnel, and simply as weeds.

Agricultural weeds are found in several verses in the Old Testament (Job 31:40; Proverbs 24:31; Hosea 10:4). Weeding of crops, however, is not mentioned in the Bible and was apparently not practiced in grain crops in Egypt.[1] This seems strange in the context of modern agriculture, where weeds are seen as competitors of the grain. But in semi-arid regions the weeds also have value as fodder and fuel. The weeds were simply allowed to mature with the crop, like the tares, and were used to feed animals or to burn. Recent archaeological work in western Iran documents the use of weeds as fuel.[2]

The two most likely candidates for tares are common segetals (weeds associated with crops) in the Middle East. The first is Syrian cephalaria,[3] related to the attractive garden scabiosa, grown for their colorful flowers (actually aggregations of flowers) and decorative fruiting heads. Syrian cephalaria is restricted in its range while the other candidate, tares, is found throughout much of the world, both as a weed and a pasture crop. Few grasses are known to be toxic so it may seem surprising that tares has frequently been implicated in cattle poisoning and, rarely, human poisoning due to the presence of a toxic micro-organism that invades the plant.

Syrian cephalaria is an annual, reaching a height of 4 feet (ca. 1.3 meters) with a single stem that branches to produce numerous heads of flowers. Flowers are less attractive than many members of the family and produce a small, hard seed (technically a fruit) with a very bitter taste. In the Middle East, this plant is found in the driest places wheat is grown.

On the other hand, tares is a grass that, like Syrian cephalaria, grows to the same height as a mature wheat plant and is often found growing in wheat fields and, less frequently, in barley crops. The grains are similar in size to wheat. It is a classic segetal plant.

1. Murray, *Cereal Processing*, 520.
2. Whitlam et al., *Cutting the Mustard*, 12–13.
3. *Cephalaria syriaca*.

The association of tares with wheat requires a closer look at the only text where this plant is mentioned, Matthew 13:

> Here is another story Jesus told: "The Kingdom of Heaven is like a farmer who planted good seed in his field. But that night as the workers slept, his enemy came and planted weeds among the wheat, then slipped away. When the crop began to grow and produce grain, the weeds also grew. The farmer's workers went to him and said, 'Sir, the field where you planted that good seed is full of weeds! Where did they come from?' 'An enemy has done this!' the farmer exclaimed. 'Should we pull out the weeds?' they asked. 'No,' he replied, 'you'll uproot the wheat if you do. Let both grow together until the harvest. Then I will tell the harvesters to sort out the weeds, tie them into bundles, and burn them, and to put the wheat in the barn.'" (vv. 24–30 NIV)

Unlike any of the other six parables in this chapter, this one required unpacking by the Teacher.

> Then, leaving the crowds outside, Jesus went into the house. His disciples said, "Please explain to us the story of the weeds in the field." Jesus replied, "The Son of Man is the farmer who plants the good seed. The field is the world, and the good seed represents the people of the Kingdom. The weeds are the people who belong to the evil one. The enemy who planted the weeds among the wheat is the devil. The harvest is the end of the world, and the harvesters are the angels. Just as the weeds are sorted out and burned in the fire, so it will be at the end of the world. The Son of Man will send his angels, and they will remove from his Kingdom everything that causes sin and all who do evil. And the angels will throw them into the fiery furnace, where there will be weeping and gnashing of teeth. Then the righteous will shine like the sun in their Father's Kingdom. Anyone with ears to hear should listen and understand!" (Matthew 13:36–43 NIV)

If the parable is to be understood, we have to take a closer look at the text. First, tares are associated with wheat, not with the other dominant grain, barley. Tares, at least when found in barley, mature later and it is obvious that the weed in the parable has a life cycle that is synchronous with the wheat. Put another way, tares are segetal plants in wheat fields. When the wheat nears maturity, the weed and the wheat plants can be distinguished. How does this background help us discern which weeds in traditional (i.e., non-mechanized) wheat culture behaved like biblical tares? There is evidence from indigenous peoples.

Local Arab farmers in Jordan, Lebanon, and Syria refer to a weed known as *zawan*. This pejorative word describes an undesirable weed of wheat enshrined in a proverb, "The *zawan* of your own field is better than the wheat of the crusaders," a saying often applied by villagers seeking wives from more distant places rather than their own villages.

In Jordan, *zawan* is clearly Syrian cephalaria. Farmers state unequivocally that it occurs only in wheat, not in barley. On the other hand, farmers in higher rainfall areas of Lebanon and Syria use the term *zawan* for tares.[4]

Translating tares as "thistle," as in *The Message* translation, seems to miss the teaching of the parable that the intruder resembles or imitates the crop. This is certainly not the case with thistles.

In drier areas of the Levant, Syrian cephalaria appears to be a more common weed in wheat while tares is a more serious in wheat (and to a lesser extent barley) in areas with higher rainfall.

Figure 1. A mature tares fruiting spike. Unlike the grains that it pollutes, tares are not shattering so that the grains do not fall when disturbed ensuring the weed is harvested with the crop.

4. In one of the instances of use of tares grains, Haddad reports that they were once used as an anesthetic. Haddad, *Zuwan*.

Figure 2. Tares in a barley field east of Latakia, Syria. The green stems of the tares can be seen.

Figure 3. Syrian cephalaria at the edge of a wheat field Sulaimani Province, Kurdish Iraq.

TEREBINTH

One of the major forest types in the eastern Mediterranean region is known as the oak-terebinth forest because terebinth[1] species are important components. They can be large trees with hard durable wood valued for building and carpentry. Leaves are compound. Trees are unisexual with small, inconspicuous flowers apparently wind pollinated. Fruits are small and hard with a resinous taste.

It is unclear from the Scriptures precisely which tree is indicated by the Hebrew word *ĕlah* or one of its derivatives and it has apparently caused confusion by its similarity to *ĕlôn*, the word usually translated as oak.[2] (See Oaks.) For example, the tree under which King Saul was buried (1 Chronicles 16:12) is termed "the green tree" (NIV), "oak" (KJV, NASB), and "terebinth" (JND). In 1 Chronicles 14:14, the same tree is called "balsam" (NIV), and "mulberry" (KJV, JND). Balsam may be used as a name here because of a resin extracted from the tree. Several unrelated plants with a fragrant resin are also referred to as balsam.

What is terebinth, or more correctly, pistacia? Three species occur in the Middle East: the Atlantic pistacia,[3] terebinth,[4] and the Palestine pistacia.[5] Atlantic pistacia is the largest and therefore assumed to be the one in the Scriptures, although it is not possible to precisely determine the species.

When undisturbed (a rare occurrence in the Middle East) the trees reach a large size and can live up to one thousand years. Pistacia develops a deep and extensive root system and therefore remains green even in years of drought. It commonly sprouts from the stump after cutting,[6] as noted in Isaiah 6:13.

---

1. Terebinth trees are in the genus *Pistacia*. Because these trees have a broad distribution in varied language groups, there are numerous common names.
2. Beckmann, *Terebinth Resin*, 30 provides a helpful review of the confusion between the word used for oak and the word used for terebinth.
3. *P. atlantica*.
4. *P. terebinthus*.
5. *P. palaestina*.
6. Such basal shoot development is known as coppicing.

Additional references to pistacia are found in Genesis 35:4, Judges 6:11, 1 Chronicles 10:12, Isaiah 6:13, and Isaiah 44:14. Because of its large size and great age, pistacia trees were well-known landmarks and were used as memorials for the dead, a practice still followed in some Arab villages. But the pistacia trees could have been the object of idolatry (Hosea 4:13). Did Jacob bury the idols under the "oak" of Shechem (Genesis 35:4) because the tree was an object of veneration? Since the cultic uses of terebinths extend back to Minoan civilization, was the worship of these trees by the Israelites a continuation of a long-established practice?[7]

As often in the holy books, great trees are associated with great men. Gideon was by a large pistacia when he was called by God (Judges 6:11). David faced Goliath in the Valley of the Pistacias (1 Samuel 17:2). Absalom, great in his own eyes, was trapped in a large pistacia.

Gums

Gums and resins are both plant exudates represented in a great diversity of plants. Chemically, gums are water soluble, which resins are not, though are soluble in alcohols. There are of course various combinations called gum resins. Countless people consume a product of acacia trees every day without knowing it. Just review the ingredients in ice cream and many candies and you will likely find gum arabic. Gum was used in the compounding of the sacred incense (Exodus 30:34), but we do not know the source of this gum or whether it was derived from an acacia.[8] In addition to gum arabic, trees in the genus *Acacia* are sources of foods, medicine, and timber. The only specific use for the tree documented in Scripture, however, is for construction.

One of the features of the genus *Pistacia* is the presence of resins and oils, producing a fragrant resin with a smell resembling turpentine. The source of our English word turpentine is derived from the word terebinth. In North America, turpentine is derived from pine trees,[9] but in ancient times terebinth was the source of a compound used in a similar manner. The famed balm of Gilead is a candidate for the resin of this tree. (See Balm of Gilead.)

This resin is now known to be one of the materials used in preparation of mummies in ancient Egypt.[10] Since terebinth trees are not native to Egypt, resin was imported from Gilead and contiguous regions.

7. Beckmann, *Pistacia Resin,* 57–62.
8. Another candidate for the source of gum is *Astragalus tragacanthus,* gum tragacanth.
9. Chiefly from longleaf pine, *Pinus palustris.*
10. Buckley and Evershed, *Embalming Agents.*

The small, hard fruits of Palestine terebinth are sold in Arab markets as a condiment and are sometimes a component of *zaatar*, a spicy mix put on hot bread. The flavor reminds me of pine resin.

The appellation of balm to the exudate of these trees is appropriate since they have been used as medicine since time immemorial and at present terebinth preparations are being studied for their medical efficacy.[11]

Figure 1. Atlantic pistacia with developing fruit, Sidi Bou Ghaba Preserve, Morocco.

Figure 2. Atlantic Pistacia in flower, Chouf, Mount Lebanon.

11. Milia et al., *Preparations of Pistacia*.

TEREBINTH 269

Figure 3. Mastic, Chios, Greece. This is the source of the highly valued mastic resin.

Figure 4. Atlantic pistacia south of Kufur Yusef, Galilee, Israel. A local Palestinian told me the cloth hung on the tree was to honor a deceased "holy person." Trees decorated with such cloths or with ribbons are frequent in Muslim areas.

Figure 5. Palestine terebinth, Mount Tabor, Israel. This species is smaller and less frequent that the Atlantic terebinth.

THISTLE

In much of the Middle East, thistles are the most conspicuous vegetation along roads and in fields. At the edge of barley and wheat fields, a painful border of thistles guards the harvest. In fact, thistles and other armed plants are so common in this part of the world that if you sent a first-time visitor on a hike through fields, he/she would quickly get the point!

No wonder these succulent and often delicious plants need protection. The entire countryside, including urban areas, is grazed by goats and sheep. If a plant is not toxic nor armed, it ends up as a meal! So, not surprisingly, thistles are common.

The Scriptures do not discriminate between thorns and thistles, a reflection of the taxonomy of utility of the ancients. In the first reference to armed plants in the Bible we read, "It [the cursed ground] will produce thorns and thistles for you, and you will eat the plants of the field" (Genesis 3:18 NIV).

The Genesis account is a helpful commentary on the ecology of thistles. They are usually associated with disturbed areas like fields and roadsides. Scripture provides several examples. "I went past the field of the sluggard, past the vineyard of the man who lacks judgment; thorns had come up everywhere, the ground was covered with weeds, and the stone wall was in ruins" (Proverbs 24:30 NIV). These "thorns" are probably thistles, as a woody plant would not grow as fast as an annual plant. Thistles are annual, armed plants.

The leaf-like structures that surround the flower head of one of the best-known thistles, the garden artichoke,[1] are tipped with a sharp point. These are removed until the immature flower head remains, the heart of the artichoke. Wild relatives of the cultivated artichoke[2] are common in the Middle East and often have horrific prickles on the flower head 3 centimeters (about 1.5 inches) long. Despite recommendations of colleagues who foraged, the armament discouraged me from testing the culinary value of the plant! When young, the flower heads of the wild artichoke resemble an old-fashioned shaving brush, giving it one of its common names in Arabic,

1. *Cynara cardunculus* var. *scolymus,* known in English as cardoon.
2. *Cynara cardunculus* var. *cardunculus.*

"the donkey's shaving brush" (so called for its brush-like flowers and impressive armor).

Thistles are non-woody plants that are outfitted with prickles, one of the three different kinds of plant armor recognized by botanists.[3] Whatever they are called, a personal encounter with a thorn, spine, or prickle can be painful.

Perhaps it is because thistles are often annual plants that need to protect themselves, even at the youngest stages, that they have prickles. Thorns and spines are most common on trees and shrubs or perennial plants. Prickles are formed on the leaves, stems, and even the flower heads while the plants are young—and most susceptible to grazing.

Individual flowers of the sunflower family are very small, seldom more than a few millimeters wide. But hundreds can be produced in a solitary flowering head. Each flower produces a single seeded fruit, commonly referred to as a seed. Fruits may have specialized adaptations for airborne dispersal. Long soft hairs ("down") allow the fruits to be lifted by the dry winds of summer and widely scattered. I am always intrigued at the incongruity of soft thistle down caught in the sharp prickles of the plant. Seeds of many thistles can remain dormant in the soil so that when the area is plowed or disturbed, the seeds are exposed to light and water and then germinate.

There are many thistles in the flora and I have selected only a few that are common to show their weaponry, diversity, and beauty.

---

3. Thorns are modified branches. Spines are modified leaves. Prickles are sharp projections that arise for any plant surface.

Figure 1. A species of cottonthistle,[4] Chios, Greece.

4. *Onopordum acanthium*. Tentative determination.

Figure 2. Small globe thistle,[5] Mateppe, Istanbul, Turkey.[6]

5. *Echinops minima.*
6. Despite their often-aggressive weediness in Western Asia, several species are garden subjects readily available from nurseries in the United States.

Figure 3. Flowering head of small globe thistle showing the individual star-like flowers.

Figure 4. Yellow star thistle[7] has become a noxious weed in Mediterranean climates around the world. Note the toothpick sized thorns. Campus of the American University of Iraq-Sulaimani.

Figure 5. Flowering head of milk thistle with prodigious deterrents to predators of the edible inner part of the head.

7. *Centaurea solstitialis.*

Figure 6. Milk thistle[8] near Antakya, Turkey. It is called milk thistle because the white splotches on the leaves look like spilled milk. There is a recent review of its uses and history.[9]

8. *Silybum marianum*. This is very popular in herbal medicine; the seeds and concoctions of the leaves and other plant parts are widely sold.

9. Porwal et al., *Milk Thistle*.

THYINE

The Bible describes many items of high value. Most are well known—gold, silver, various gemstones. Lesser known is thyine,[1] a plant found in only one verse: "She [Babylon] bought great quantities of gold, silver, jewels, and pearls; fine linen, purple, silk, and scarlet cloth; things made of fragrant thyine wood, ivory goods, and objects made of expensive wood; and bronze, iron, and marble" (Revelation 18:11–12 NLT).

These luxury goods, including thyine wood, were traded in Babylon, a city symbolic of materialism and hedonism. "Thyine" is the transliteration of the Greek *thuinos* and therefore the translation preferred over "citron wood" (NIV, NKJV), "perfumed wood" (NLT), or "scented wood" (RSV).

Thyine wood was well known in the ancient Mediterranean world. It is one of the most beautiful woods in the world. People living in New Testament times would recognize thyine as a wood used to make furniture for the rich and powerful, consonant with its inclusion in a list of luxury items. As Pliny the Elder put it so clearly: "Few things that supply the apparatus of a more luxurious life rank with this tree."[2] He wrote that the outstanding feature of the wood—derived, as he rightly notes, from the underground portion of the tree—had "wavy marks forming a vein or else little spirals"; and, "Some have wavy crinkled markings, which are more esteemed if they resemble the eyes in a peacock's tail."[3] In Homer's *Odyssey*, the alluring Calypso burns thyine in her fireplace, which is referred to by Pliny in his review of the tree's history. As they are today, beautiful tables were inlaid with thyine; Pliny recorded one that was sold at the price of a large estate.[4]

The thyine tree is a small gymnosperm native to North Africa. Theophrastus noted it growing in the district of Cyrene, modern-day Libya, where it was extirpated by overharvesting and urban sprawl. Today, the

1. *Tetraclinis articulata.*
2. Rackham, *Pliny thyine*, 159.
3. Rackham, *Pliny Thyine*, 157.
4. Pliny writes: "The natives bury the timber in the ground while still green, giving it a coat of wax; but carpenters lay it in heaps of corn for periods of a week with intervals of a week between, and it is surprising how much its weight is reduced by this process." Rackham, *Pliny Thyine*, 157. This is a bewildering process for an undescribed purpose. Pliny states that one benefit of thyine tables is resistance to wine.

largest stands of are found in the Atlas Mountains of Morocco, with outlier populations in Algeria, Spain, and a small stand in Malta. About 10 percent of present forest cover in Morocco is thyine, known in Moroccan Arabic as *araar*; most of this forest is on government land. The center of the *araar* industry is the city of Essaouira on the Atlantic Ocean, with the largest extant trees being in the vicinity of Agadir in southern Morocco.

Two types of wood are extracted from the tree. The choice wood is from the underground portion, where numerous buds create a bird's-eye pattern. The aerial portion of the tree provides timber that is easy to work, strong, but unremarkable in color.

The tree can reach a height of 10 meters (30 feet), with a crown typical of many gymnosperms—conical when mature. Pollen cones and seed cones are produced on the same tree. An unusual feature of thyine culture is coppicing: the stems are cut and the trees resprout from the root.

Resin, known as sandarac, is extracted from the tree. The resin is implied in the translation of thyine as "fragrant wood" in some Bible versions. Stems are incised, allowing the resin to exude and harden; it is then collected. This practice of cutting the trees to extract sandarac was outlawed in Morocco more than fifty years ago. Sandarac was used in preparing mummies and was widely traded in ancient times.

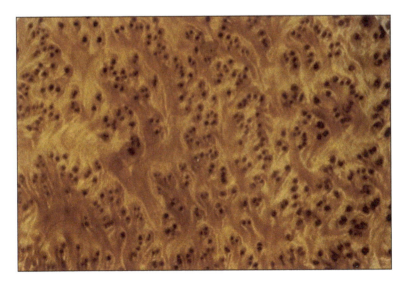

Figure 1. Section of thyine root showing the attractive birds-eye pattern.

Figure 2. Stand of thyine trees Tamara, Morocco.

Figure 3. Sandarac resin, derived from thyine trees. The government of Morocco has proscribed the harvest and sale of the resin.

TUMBLEWEED

Tumbleweed[1] *is a common* plant in the steppe regions of Bible lands known locally in Arabic as *akoub* and valued as a vegetable. Some scholars think that the tumbleweed of Psalm 83:13—"Make them like tumbleweed, O my God, like chaff before the wind" (NIV)—is this plant. The reference in the Bible does not refer to its gustatory use, but rather to the tumbling nature of the plant similar in mechanism to the famous tumbleweeds of the American Great Plains. Unlike the American traveling plant, *akoub* is a thistle.

In common with all thistles, this is a heavily armed plant. In March plants are cut at the base and the prickles removed. The disarmed plants are relished as a delicacy that is cooked with meat or sauteed with oil and onions. I purchased some in Jordan from a young Bedouin boy selling along a country road. Tediously, I removed the young but strong prickles with scissors. Then, I cooked them with a little olive oil. The flavor resembled mild broccoli. Like so many wild foods, their desirability resides in their wild origin and lore more than any outstanding flavor. Harvesting has become so widespread that measures are being taken to protect the plant in some countries.[2] After my experience preparing the delicacy ending with bloody hands from all the prickles and resulting in only a few bits to eat, I certainly pose no threat to populations of *akoub*.

The seeds (technically fruits) are roasted and sold as a snack. I have purchased them in the bazaar in Sulaimani, in Kurdish Iraq. While it is frustrating to get the meat from the seed, it is tasty, resembling sunflower seeds, especially when roasted.

By mid-May, the stem has separated from the root, allowing the entire plant to be carried by the wind. The specialized mechanism involves the abscission of the entire stem from the base of the plant, a process timed to take advantage of the dry winds that arise in the late spring and summer.

Near Makawir, the location of Herod's palace east of the Jordan and the likely site of the decapitation of John the Baptist I found abundant *akoub* preparing for its journey across the steppe. As the thistle tumbles over the open ground, the fruits fall out, ensuring distribution at a distance from

1. *Gundelia tournefortii*.
2. Hind, *Gundelia Tournefortii*, 132.

the mother plant. *Akoub's* dispersal takes place at about the same time as the wheat harvest, perhaps suggested by the prophet Isaiah: "driven before the wind like chaff on the hills, like tumbleweed before a gale" (17:14 NIV).

Figure 1. Tumbleweed blown along road at Mukawir, Jordan.

Figure 2. Flowering *akoub* past the stage for harvesting. Kartak, Kurdish Iraq.

TUMBLEWEED 283

Figure 3. Young *akoub* plants in the market in Irbil, Kurdish Iraq.

Figure 4. Seeds, technically fruits, of *akoub* from the bazaar in Sulaimani, Kurdish Iraq. Like the other food prepared from this thistle, considerable effort is required to extricate the small quantity of food. The seeds taste like sunflower seeds.

WALNUT

The nuts of the English walnut[1] are common in America at Christmas time, when they are more popular than our native, but more flavorful, black walnut[2] because they are much easier to crack. Like black walnut, the wood of English walnut is highly valued and is one of the woods used in the beautiful damascene furniture in which mother-of-pearl is inlaid into the walnut. But the walnut in the single reference in the Bible is included not because of its wood nor directly because of its nuts but because of its symbolism in fertility.

Scholars agree that the nut trees mentioned in Song of Songs 6:11 are English walnuts cultivated extensively in many parts of the world.[3] The center of origin of this species is not known, but it is widely grown in the Middle East where the seeds of the fruits ("nuts") are eaten.

The walnut is a large, graceful tree. The dark green leaves would drop at the end of the growing season, and the strong thick trunk would tower over the vines and the shrubby pomegranates of Solomon's garden, a garden associated with fertility. In ancient times, the walnut was a symbol of fertility, so it would be fitting in such a garden.

There are two gardens in Song of Songs 6. The first is in verse 2 and is a garden of spices and lilies, here the ambience is sensuous, redolent, colorful. Verse 11 is a garden of nuts, located in the valley and associated with grapes and pomegranates, with a theme of fertility.

---

1. *Juglans regia,* also known as Persian walnut.
2. *Juglans nigra.*
3. Langgut, *Prestigious Fruit Trees,* 101.

WALNUT 285

Figure 1. Walnuts in the bazaar in Sulaimani, Kurdish Iraq.

Figure 2. Developing walnuts, Chios, Greece.

WATERMELON

"*We remember the fish* we ate in Egypt that cost nothing, the cucumbers, the melons, the leeks, the onions and the garlic" (Numbers 11:5 ESV).

It is counter intuitive, but watermelon is a desert as well as a dessert plant and has been cultivated in North Africa for millennia.[1] While there is little disagreement over the translation, there is debate over the provenance of watermelon, whether it is native to southern Africa or to the Sahara region.[2] The report of five-thousand-year-old watermelon seeds from Libya supports the autochthonicity of watermelon in the Sahara.[3]

One of the most familiar of all summer fruits in many parts of the world, watermelon is an annual vine grown for its fruits and seeds. Watermelon seeds are not well known as a food in the United States, but some cultivars are grown exclusively in Egypt and Western Asia to produce this common snack. Dried and roasted the seeds add considerably to the nutritional value of the crop because of the oil content of the seeds. A wax can also be extracted from the rinds. The Numbers text does not indicate how the children of Israel used watermelon, but it is reasonable that they used it for more than its flesh.

The citron, not mentioned in the Bible but widely referred in Jewish literature, is a kind of watermelon.[4] The name is also applied to a type of citrus fruit for its flavoring and oil rather than a comestible.[5]

---

1. *Citrullus lanatus.*

2. Zohary et al., *Domestication*, 154–55. Paris, *Dessert Watermelon* provides evidence of the development of the sweet-fleshed watermelon in the Sahara region and disputes the theory that it originally came from southern Africa.

3. Wasylikowa and van der Veen, *Watermelon History,* 216–17.

4. *Citrullus lanatus* var. *citroides.*

5. *Citrus medica.*

Figure 1. Desert watermelon,[6] ancestor to the dessert watermelon. Namib Desert, Namibia.

Figure 2. Opened desert melon to show the preponderance of seeds rather than juicy flesh. As noted above, some varieties are grown for the edible seeds, still an important crop in North Africa and the Middle East.

6. *Citrullus lanatus.*

Figure 3. Melon or colycinth mosaic, Medaba, Jordan.

WHEAT

Wheat is the first of the seven species of the land of Canaan (Deuteronomy 8:8). It was the source of the most important food, providing most of the calories for the inhabitants of the land. There are more than 325 references to bread in the Bible, all but a few referring to wheaten bread.

But there are numerous other uses for wheat, essential in an agrarian society, including production of beer, basketry, a source of temper for making bricks, and fodder. All parts of the wheat plant were valued—the grain, the stalks, and the byproducts of grain production.

Wheat has the distinction of being a crop that is considerably different in its present form than it was in Bible days. Knowing this difference helps understand some verses that would not be clear without knowing this difference. The evolution of wheat is a classic example of crop evolution reviewed elsewhere.[1]

The type of wheat grown in Bible days was all durum wheat, when ground with the bran and germ removed known as semolina. Durum wheat differs genetically and nutritionally from bread wheat, the most widely grown wheat today.[2] There is a difference in the amount of gluten found in the two types of wheat. Bread wheat has considerable gluten so that the bread rises to produce the traditional fluffy loaf. Durum wheat, on the other hand, has less gluten and therefore does not rise as much in baking, forming the characteristic flatter breads of indigenous peoples in the Middle East. Virtually no bread wheat was grown in Bible times.[3]

The only kind of wheat known from ancient Egypt is emmer wheat.[4] With an increased understanding of the kinds of ancient wheats, it is not surprising that the English Standard Version uses emmer, but unfortunately misapplied it in the account of the plague of hail in Egypt called by Moses: "The flax and the barley were struck down, for the barley was in the ear and

---

1. Musselman, *Plants*, 291–92. For more detail on wheat evolution, see Zohary et al., *Domestication*, 23–51.

2. Van Sladen and Payne, *Wheat Nomenclature*. This is a helpful update in the taxonomy of wheats and further iterations will undoubtably appear.

3. Zohary et al., *Domestication*, 41–45.

4. Samuel, *Amarna*.

the flax was in bud. But the wheat and the emmer were not struck down, for they are late in coming up" (Exodus 9:31–32 ESV). The wheat *was* emmer wheat so that a different plant is indicated by the word translated by the ESV as emmer.

Two types of durum wheat were grown, each recognized by how the grain is borne in relation to the scale-like coverings or hulls called bracts. In hulled wheats, the grain is retained within the bracts and needs to be removed before grinding. The other wheat is not hulled and known as free-threshing wheat; grains are easily removed upon threshing.

Threshing is one of the stages in the wheat harvest. After cutting (or pulling of the entire plant, a means of increasing the fodder value) the grain is threshed. In free threshing wheat this yields grains while in hulled wheat the grain remains covered with the bracts. Winnowing—the separation of the grain from the attending bracts—yields grain in free threshing varieties but is only one of several steps in preparing emmer. The product of winnowing is chaff (see below) and the grain is then ready for storage and use.

The resulting product is whole grain, a whole grain flour which like modern whole wheat flour cannot be stored for a long time because the embryo, the germ, contains oils that can become rancid with storage.

Grinding was usually done with a hand mill, which had to be used each time flour was needed. Knowing this helps explain such passages as Deuteronomy 24:6 "Do not take a pair of millstones—not even the upper one—as security for a debt, because that would be taking a man's livelihood as security" (NIV).

Emmer wheat, durum wheat that is hulled, requires an additional step in its preparation. Before the hulled wheat could be ground, it first had to have the hulls removed. This was done using a mortar and pestle or by extended threshing with oxen. An obscure verse in Micah 4:13 may refer to this added step: "Rise and thresh, Daughter Zion, for I will give you horns of iron; I will give you hooves of bronze" (NIV). These bronze (or copper) shoes for the oxen apparently increased the efficiency of threshing with draft animals.[5]

The use of mortars and pestles informs the reading of Proverbs 27:22 "Though you grind a fool in a mortar, grinding him like grain with a pestle, you will not remove his folly from him" (NIV). This is not the kind of mortar and pestle used in kitchens or often displayed at pharmacies, but rather a large wooden mortar and wooden pestle, like those still seen in many African countries for pounding grain. The use of mortar and pestles in the

---

5. Hillman, *Glume Wheats*, 123. Hillman's exhaustive treatment is the best explication of the entire process of growing glume wheats, from preparation of the field to production of foods.

preparation of emmer and other kinds of wheat in ancient Western Asia is well documented.[6]

Chaff and Brick Fine

Products from the wheat plant other than the grain are also mentioned in the Bible. One of the best known is chaff, the tiny flower parts, the bracts, that surround the grain and are removed by winnowing and, in the case of hulled emmer wheat, grinding. The most familiar chaff reference is in Psalm 1 with its contrast between the righteous and the ungodly man "And he shall be like a tree planted by the rivers of water, that bringeth forth his fruit in his season; his leaf also shall not wither; and whatsoever he doeth shall prosper. The ungodly are not so: but are like the chaff which the wind driveth away" (KJV). An additional dozen or so verses have the same imagery—chaff is a worthless material, only good for burning.

That said, chaff does have some value, both from wheat and barley, for temper in the production of bricks.[7] It was the shortage of temper for bricks which caused the children of Israel so much hardship in the account in Exodus 5. Chaff as well as straw was used for temper, as it is today. Ancient chaff is now valued. Its inclusion in ancient bricks allows botanists to determine which grain, barley or wheat (and which type of wheat), was used in manufacture. This in turn gives an indication of the kind of crops that were grown.[8]

Roasted Grain

Like beer, roasted grain (KJV "parched corn") is a lesser-known Bible wheat product. Could it be *frikeh*? Throughout modern-day northern Syria, *frikeh*[9] is a traditional way to eat wheat. *Frikeh* is made only from wheat with green heads. Dried for at least two hours after cutting, the wheat is then burned until the chaff is black, and the tip of the grain is charred. Barley is harvested at the same time as *frikeh* production, so barley straw was readily available as a fuel as it has a higher caloric value than wheat.[10] As soon as it

6. Ebeling, *Stone Tools*; Hillman, *Glume Wheats*, 129.
7. Homsher, *Mud Bricks*, 3.
8. Van der Veen, *Chaff*.
9. Ahmad and Askari, *Hawraman Frikeh*, 87. This is the only reference I know of non-Levantine frikeh.
10. Hillman, *Glume Wheats*, 142.

is cool enough to handle, the grains are removed from the heads for tasting. The soft, green grains are chewy, slightly sweet, with a desirable smokey taste. When fresh, the *frikeh* can be cooked with meat, like rice. It is usually dried, however, and ground because grinding shortens the cooking time. Drying is in the shade to avoid bleaching the green grains. Traditionally, durum wheat is used to make *frikeh* but bread wheat is also used. In Bible days, emmer was used as it was grown almost exclusively.

Could *frikeh* be the roasted or parched grain mentioned in the Bible? In the widely used Van Dyck edition of the Arabic Bible (1865), parched corn (KJV) or roasted grain (NIV) is translated *frikeh* in the six verses where it occurs.

Frikeh is a good candidate for roasted grain because of its association with the barley harvest and its use as a dried provision. In Ruth, the roasted corn was eaten at the barley harvest, which is the time that *frikeh* is prepared. In the references in 1 and 2 Samuel, roasted grain is associated with other dried foods (beans, raisins) that can be readily transported.

The word in Joshua 5:11 is different. The New Living Translation renders this as "roasted grain" but notes that it was "some of the produce of the land." In other words, this was not grain that had been brought across the Jordan. Could this be fresh *frikeh*?

Straw

Straw was used much as it is today—for animal bedding and fodder, as in Genesis 24 where Rebekah tells the servant of Abraham that both fodder and straw is available. Straw was also used to make baskets. While this industry is not explicit in the Scriptures, there is abundant historical evidence of the production of baskets and mats from straw, seldom seen in the modern Middle East.[11]

Wheat could have been used in the production of beer, but in most cases, barley was the grain of choice because barley made an inferior bread. (See Barley.)

The cropping cycle of wheat is instructive in understanding the seasons in some biblical passages. For example, "Now stand here and see the great thing the LORD is about to do. You know that it does not rain at this time of the year during the wheat harvest. I will ask the LORD to send thunder and rain today. Then you will realize how wicked you have been in asking the LORD for a king!" (1 Samuel 12:16 NLT). Rain would be unusual

---

11. I searched in several markets in the Middle East and found only one vendor of straw baskets, in Damascus.

in late May-early June when wheat is harvested. Likewise, the fruiting of mandrakes would coincide with wheat harvest, in late May or early June, as in the story of Reuben and the mandrakes (Genesis 30:14).

The best-known New Testament story of wheat sowing is the parable of the tares in Matthew 13. (See Tares.) What is seldom understood from this story is that burning the weeds was a common practice, as burning of weeds is today in parts of Syrian Mesopotamia where locals collect weeds for fuel.[12] In other words, consigning the weeds to burning more likely refers to the weeds' low value rather than intense judgement.

Figure 1. Wheat harvest near Medaba, Jordan. These workers are pulling rather than cutting the wheat.

---

12. Van der Veen, *Chaff*, 213

Figure 2. Traditional threshing of wheat using oxen in Ethiopia.

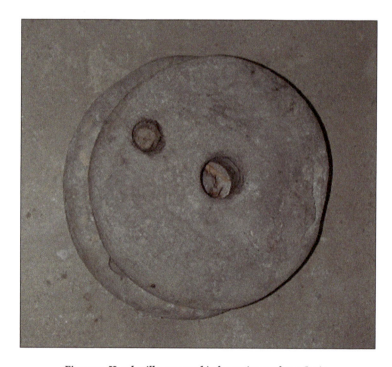

Figure 3. Hand mill preserved in home in northern Syria.

WHEAT 295

Figure 4. Close up of a sun-dried brick showing the parts of the straw and chaff used as fine. Ruins of Ebla, an Amorite city in present day northern Syria destroyed in about 2000 BC.

Figure 5. Emmer wheat in research plot, International Center for Agricultural Research in the Dry Areas, Tel Hadya, Syria.

Figure 6. Emmer wheat, upper; hard red bread wheat lower.

Figure 7. Collecting green durum wheat for preparing *frikeh*. Sair, near Hebron.

Figure 8. Flaming wheat to prepare *frikeh*. Near Idlib, Syria.

Figure 9. *Frikeh* drying on sidewalk in Aleppo. This method explains why pieces of stone turn up in purchases.

WILLOW

"*Weeping willow*"[1] *is a* misnomer for willows in the Bible. In fact, weeping willow is not even native to Western Asia. There are several species of willow in the Middle East. The Bible does not indicate which species are meant. Willows are much branched shrubs with narrow, pointed leaves, lighter on the bottom surface. Each shrub is unisexual, i.e., either male or female. The flowers are inconspicuous and borne in the spring. Seeds are equipped with hairs that enable them to float through the air ensuring dispersal. For centuries the bark of the willow has been used as a medicine and it is from the willow bark that aspirin was first extracted.

Willows are common along permanent watercourses and form dense thickets on the banks of the Jordan, especially in its upper reaches. These denizens of streambanks are mentioned in only four places: Leviticus 23:40, Job 40:22, Isaiah 15:7, and Isaiah 44:4.

In Scripture, the willow is always associated with a brook or river, that is, with a perpetual source of nourishment and supply. This application is seen in Isaiah 44:4, "And they shall spring up among the grass, as willows by the watercourses" (NIV). This is a different allusion than that in Psalm 1:3 and Jeremiah 17:8 where the emphasis is on being planted and on yielding fruit. In the case of the willow, the emphasis is on the vigor of the growth and the intimate association with the watercourse.

The wood of willow is soft and not very durable but was used in Bible days for miscellaneous bowls, other utensils, and some construction.[2] While the wood is considered poor quality, the narrow stems or withes are still used to make baskets. One of the traditional uses of willow wood in Syria is for crafting forms for darning clothing. Willow wood is cut into egg-shaped structures that will fit into a sock and easily absorb mis-directed needle points.

1. *Salix babylonica.*
2. Gale et al., *Egyptian Wood.*

Figure 1. Goat willow[3] along Lake Abant, Turkey. The lance-shaped leaves are typical of most willows. Developing, cottony fruits are in the center of the picture, indicating this as a female shrub.

---

3. *Salix caprea.*

Figure 2. Brook willow[4] along the Tigris River, northeastern Syria.

Figure 3. White willow,[5] along tributary of the Tigris River, Chami Razan, Kurdish Iraq.

4. *Salix acmophylla.*
5. *Salix alba.*

WORMWOOD

Wormwood is enigmatic and we should not be surprised that we cannot with certainty determine the plant indicated by the Hebrew in the seven verses where it occurs. However, since it is linked with gall (see Gall) in two instances perhaps two different plants are meant. The biblical texts suggest that the plant in question should be a bitter plant, be capable of being made into a decoction, and be drunk without poisoning (i.e., Jeremiah 9:15; 23:15).

In the New Testament wormwood is found only in Revelation 8:11, where a star is called Wormwood. The Greek word implies a bitter or poisonous plant. This verse clearly states that some who drank of the wormwood died, suggesting that it is toxic. Of course, we must consider the highly symbolic imagery of Revelation before trying to assign a botanical name to the wormwood.

What native plant in the Middle East conforms to the characteristics of wormwood in the Bible? Most studies on Bible plants implicate a woody shrub in the sunflower family known in English as wormwood.[1] Wormwood has been known as a medicine since ancient times. A decoction of the leaves is used to cure intestinal worms, hence the common name. Today it is seldom used for its antihelminthic properties, though it is still drunk.

A flavoring for alcoholic drinks is made from wormwood and known in English as absinthe, directly derived from the Greek word used in the New Testament (*apsinthion*). It is also known as "bitters" for obvious reasons. It has an intensely bitter taste, which probably adds to its desirability as a medicine, with the philosophy that anything that tastes that bad must be good for you!

---

1. *Artemisia herbaalba.*

WORMWOOD 303

Figure 1. Steppe near Palmyra, Syria, where grazing has reduced the wormwood to nubbins.

Figure 2. The silver-grey foliage characterizes this important fodder plant.

References Cited

Abu Alwafa, Reem. "*Origanum syriacum* L. (za'atar), From Raw to Go: A Review." *Plants* 10 (2021) 1–10.

Ahmad, Saman A., and Askari, Ali A. "Ethnobotany of the Hawraman Region of Kurdistan Iraq." *Harvard Papers in Botany* 20.1 (2015) 85–89.

Alizoti, Paraskevi, et al. "Mediterranean Firs *Abies* spp." *EUFORGEN Technical Guidelines for Genetic Conservation and Use of Mediterranean Firs* (Abies spp.). Rome: International Plant Genetic Resources Institute, 2009.

Allaby, Robin G., et al. "Evidence of the Domestication of Flax (*Linum usitatissimum* L.) from Genetic Diversity of the sad2 Locus." *Theoretical and Applied Genetics* 112 (2015) 58–65.

Álvarez-Mon, Javier. "The Introduction of Cotton into the Near East: A View from Elam." *International Journal of the Society of Iranian Archeology* 1.2 (2015) 1–17.

Andrews, Alfred C. "The Use of Rue as a Spice by the Greeks and Romans." *The Classical Journal* 43.6 (1948) 371–73.

Anonymous. *The Periplus of the Erythraean Sea: Travel and Trade in the Indian Ocean by a Merchant of the First Century*. Translated by Wilfred H. Schoff. Reprint, New York: Longmans, 1912.

Arbel, Yoav. "Olive Oil Soap in the Holy Land: Background Technology and a Newly Discovered Workshop in Jaffa." *Industrial Archaeology Review* 43.1 (2021) 54–64.

Arora, Vivek, et al. "Wild Coriander: An Untapped Genetic Resource for Future Coriander Breeding." *Euphytica* 138 (2021) 1–11.

Arunkumar, A. N., and Geeta Joshi. "*Pterocarpus santalinus* (Red Sanders) an Endemic, Endangered Tree of India: Current Status, Improvement, and the Future." *Journal of Tropical Forestry and the Environment* 4.2 (2014) 1–10.

el Bahri, S. et al. *Retama raetam* W [sic]: "A Poisonous Plant of North Africa." *Veterinary and Human Toxicology* 41.1 (1999) 33–35.

Barreca, Davide, et al. "Almonds (*Prunus dulcis* (Mill.) D. A. Webb): A Source of Nutrients and Health-Promoting Compounds." *Nutrients* 12.3 (2020) https://doi.org/10.3390/nu12030672

Basal, Nasir. "Aspects of the Biblical Material World in Medieval Judeo-Arabic: Flora and Fauna in Abū al-Faraj Hārūn's Glossary Šarḥ al Alfāẓal al-Ṣa'ba fī al-Miqra to Isaiah." *Miscelánea de Estudios Árabes y Hebraicos. Sección Hebreo* 69 (2020) 9–29.

Basson, Alex. "'People Are Plants'—A Conceptual Metaphor in the Hebrew Bible." *Old Testament Essays. Journal of the Old Testament Society of South Africa.* 19.2 (2006) 573–83.

Beckmann, Sabine. "Resin and Ritual Purification: Terebinth in Eastern Mediterranean Bronze Age Cult." In *Athanasia: The Earthly, the Celestial and the Underworld in the Mediterranean from the Late Bronze and the Early Iron Age*, edited by Nikolaos Chr. Stampolidēs et al., 29–42. Proceedings of the IVth International Congress of Ethnobotany, Yeditepe University, Istanbul 2005. Hereklion, Greece: University of Crete, 2012.[1]

Ben-Yehoshua, Shimshon, et al. "Frankincense, Myrrh and Balm of Gilead: Ancient Spices of Southern Arabia and Judea." *Horticultural Reviews* 39 (2012) 1–76.

Besnard, Guillaume, et al. "On the Origins and Domestication of the Olive: A Review and Perspective." *Annals of Botany* 121 (2018) 385–403.

Blaise, Desouza. "Effect of Tillage Systems on Weed Control, Yield and Fibre Quality of Upland (*Gossypium hirsutum* L.) and Asiatic Tree Cotton (*G. arboreum* L.)." *Soil and Tillage Research* 91 (2006) 207–16.

Bodoni Semwal, Ruchi, et al. "*Lawsonia inermis* L. (Henna): Ethnobotanical, Phytochemical and Pharmacological Aspects." *Journal of Ethnopharmacology* 155 (2014) 80–103.

Boskabadi, Javad, et al. "Mild-to-Severe Poisoning Due to *Conium maculatum* as Toxic Herb: A Case Study." *Clinical Case Reports* 9 (2021) e04509.

Bosse-Griffiths, Kate. "The Fruit of the Mandrake in Egypt and Israel." In *Amarna Studies and Other Selected Papers*, edited by J. Gwynn Griffiths, 82–96. Göttingen: Vandenhoeck and Ruprecht, 2001.

Bouchard, Charlène, et al. "Cotton Cultivation and Textile Production in the Arabian Peninsula during Antiquity: The Evidence from Madâ'in Sâlih (Saudi Arabia) and Qal'at al-Bahrain (Bahrain)." *Vegetation History and Archaeobotany* 20.5 (2011) 405–17.

Boulos, Loutfy. *Flora of Egypt. Volume Three, Verbenaceae-Compositae*. Cairo: Al Hadara, 2002.

Braimbridge, Mark V. "Boxwood in Biblical Times." *Topiarius* 10 (2006) 7–9.

———. "Boxwood in Roman Times. Part I: *Buxus*—The Plant." *Topiarius* 12 (2008) 14–16.

———. "Boxwood in Roman Times. Part II: *Buxus*—The Wood & Its Uses." *Topiarius* 12 (2009) 14–18.

Brite, Elizabeth Baker. "The Origins of the Apple in Central Asia." *Journal of World Prehistory* 34 (2021) 159–93.

Buckley, Steven A., and Richard P. Evershed. "Organic Chemistry of Embalming Agents in Pharaonic and Graeco-Roman Mummies." *Nature* 413.6858 (2001) 837–42.

Caseau, Beatrice. "Incense and Fragrances: From House to Church. A Study of the Introduction of Incense in the Early Byzantine Christian Churches." In *Material Culture and Well-being in Byzantium (400–1453)*, edited by Michael Grünbart et al., 72–92. Proceedings of the International Conference. Vienna: Austrian Academy of Sciences, 2007.

Chao, ChihCheng T., and Robert R. Krueger. "The Date Palm (*Phoenix dactylifera* L.): Overview of Biology, Uses and Cultivation." *HortScience* 42.5 (2007) 1077–82.

Cheng, Zhuo, et al. "From Folk Taxonomy to Species Confirmation of Acorus (Acoraceae): Evidences Based on Phylogenetic and Metabolomic Analyses." *Frontiers in Plant Science* 11 (2020). doi.org/10.3389/fpls.2020.00965.

---

1. Much of this paper was published elsewhere; this is the latest edition I have found.

Company, Rafel S. I., et al. "Taxonomy, Botany, and Physiology." In *Almonds: Botany, Production and Uses,* edited by Rafel S. I. Company and Thomas M. Gradziel, 1–42. Wallingford UK: CABI, 2017.
Coles, Peter. *Mulberry.* London: Reaktion, 2019.
Cooke, William D., et al. "The Hand-Spinning of Ultrafine Yarns, Part 2. The Spinning of Flax." *Bulletin du Centre International d'Ètude des Textiles Anciens* 69 (1991) 17–23.
Cornara, Laura, et al. "Comparative and Functional Screening of Three Species Traditionally Used as Antidepressants *Valeriana officinalis* L., *Valeriana jatamansi* Jones ex Roxb. and *Nardostachys jatamansi* (D. Don) DC." *Plants* 9.8.994 (2020) 1–27.
Crowfoot, Grace M., and Louise Baldensperger. "Hyssop." *Palestine Exploration Fund* (1931) 89–98.
Custódio, Valdir F. Velga-Junior. "True and Common Balsams." *Brazilian Journal of Pharmacognosy* 22.6 (2012) 1372–83.
Dafni, Amots, et al. "Myrtle, Basil, Rosemary, and Three-lobed Sage as Ritual Plants in the Monotheistic Religions: An Historical-Ethnobotanical Comparison." *Economic Botany* 74.3 (2020) 330–55.
Dafni, Amots, and Barbara Böck. "Medicinal Plants of the Bible-Revisited." *Journal of Ethnobiology and Ethnomedicine* 15.57 (2019). DOI:10.1186/s13002-019-0338-8
Dalley, Stephanie. *The Mystery of the Hanging Garden of Babylon: An Elusive World Wonder.* Oxford: Oxford University Press, 2015.
Delplancke, Malou, et al. "Evolutionary History of Almond Tree Domestication in the Mediterranean Basin." *Molecular Ecology* 22.4 (2013) 1092–1104.
Dolara, Piero, et al. "Analgesic Effects of Myrrh." *Nature* 379 (1996) 29.
Duke, James A. *Duke's Handbook of Medicinal Plants of the Bible.* Boca Raton, FL: CRC Press, 1983.
Ebeling, Jennie. "Why Are Ground Stone Tools Found in Middle and Late Bronze Age Burials?" *Near Eastern Archaeology* 65.2 (2002) 149–51.
Eickhorst, Kimberly, et al. "Rue the Herb: *Ruta graveolens*-Associated Phytophototoxicity." *Dermatitis* 18.1 (2007) 52–55.
Engel, Thomas, and Wolfgang Frey. "Fuel Resources for Copper Smelting in Antiquity in Selected Woodlands in the Edom Highlands to the Wadi Arabah Jordan." *Flora* 191 (1996) 29–39.
Fady, Bruno, et al. "Aleppo and Brutia Pines *Pinus halepensis/Pinus brutia*." *EUFORGEN Technical Guidelines for Genetic Conservation and Use of Aleppo Pine* (Pinus halepensis) *and Brutia Pine* (Pinus brutia). Rome: International Plant Genetic Resources Institute, 2004.
———. "Italian Stone Pine *Pinus pinea*." *EUFORGEN Technical Guidelines for Genetic Conservation and Use Italian Stone Pine* (Pinus pinea). Rome: International Plant Genetic Resources Institute, 2004.
Falistroco, Egizia. "The Millenary History of the Fig Tree (*Ficus carica* L.)." *Advances in Agriculture, Horticulture and Entomology* 5 (2020) 1–8.
Farjon, Aljos. *A Monograph of* Cupressaceae *and* Sciadopitys. Kew, UK: Royal Botanic Gardens, 2005.
Fleisher, Alexander, and Zhenia Fleisher. "The Fragrance of Biblical Mandrake." *Economic Botany* 48 (1995) 242–51.

Foster, Benjamin Oliver. "Notes on the Symbolism of the Apple in Classical Antiquity." *Harvard Studies in Classical Philology* 10 (1899) 39–55.

Gale, Rowena, et al. "Wood." In *Ancient Egyptian Materials and Technology*, edited by Paul T. Nicholson and Ian Shaw, 334–72. Cambridge: Cambridge University Press, 2000.

Gohari, Ahmad Reza, et al. "An Overview on Saffron, Phytochemicals, and Medicinal Properties." *Pharmacognosy Reviews* 7.13 (2013) 61–66.

Goor, Asaph. "The History of the Fig in the Holy Land from Ancient Times to the Present Day." *Economic Botany* 19.2 (1965) 124–35.

Gradziel, Thomas M. "History of Cultivation." In *Almonds: Botany, Production and Uses*, edited by Rafel S. I. Company and Thomas M. Gradziel, 43–69. Wallingford UK: CABI, 2017.

Grauso, Laura, et al. "Corn Poppy: *Papaver rheoas* L.: A Critical Review of Its Botany Phytochemistry and Pharmacology." *Phytochemical Review* 20 (2021) 227–48.

Grauso, Laura, et al. "*Urtica dioica* L.: Botanical, Phytochemical and Pharmacological Overview." *Pharmalogical Review* 19 (2020) 1341–77.

Haddad, Fouad. "Zuwan Bearded Darnel *Lolium temulentum* L. A Middle Age Arab/Islamic Anesthetic Herb." *Middle East Journal of Anaesthesiology* 18.2 (2005) 249–64.

Harrison, Roland K. "The Mandrake and the Ancient World." *The Evangelical Quarterly* 28.2 (1956) 87–92.

Hepper, F. Nigel. *Baker Encyclopedia of Bible Plants: Flowers and Trees, Fruits and Vegetables, Ecology*. Grand Rapids: Baker Book House, 1993.

Hillman, Gordon C. "Traditional Husbandry and Processing of Archaic Cereals in Recent times: The Operations, Products, and Equipment Which Might Feature in Sumerian Texts. Part I: The Glume Wheats." *Bulletin on Sumerian Agriculture* 1 (1981) 114–52.

Hind, Nicholas. "*Gundelia Tournefortii*." *Curtis Botanical Magazine* 30.2 (2013) 114–38.

Homan, Michael M. "Did the Ancient Israelites Drink Beer?" *Biblical Archaeology Review* 36.5 (2010) 1–10.

———. *To Your Tents, O Israel! The Terminology, Function, Form, and Symbolism of Tents in the Hebrew Bible and the Ancient Near East*. Leiden: Brill, 2002.

Homsher, Robert S. "Mud Bricks and the Process of Construction in the Middle Bronze Age Southern Levant." *Bulletin of the American Schools of Oriental Research* 368 (2012) 1–27.

Janick, Jules et al. "The Cucurbits of Mediterranean Antiquity: Identification of Taxa from Ancient Images and Descriptions." *Annals of Botany* 100 (2007) 1441–57.

Juniper, Barrie E., and David J. Mabberley. *The Story of the Apple*. Portland, OR: Timber, 2006.

Kahn, Lily, and Riita-Liisa Vallijärvi. "Translation of Hebrew Flora and Fauna Terminology in North Sámmi and West Greenlandic *fin de siècle* Bibles." *The Bible Translator* 70.2 (2019) 125–44.

Kaniewski, David, et al. "Primary Domestication and Early Uses of the Emblematic Olive Tree: Palaeobotanical, Historical and Molecular Evidence from the Middle East." *Biological Reviews* 87 (2012) 885–99.

Kaur, Harmeet, et al. "*Nardostachys jatamansi* (D. Don) DC: An Invaluable and Constantly Dwindling Resource of the Himalayas." *South African Journal of Botany* 135 (2020) 252–67.

Kawami, Trudy S. "Archaeological Evidence for Textiles in Pre-Islamic Iran." *Iranian studies* 25.1/2 (1992) 7–8.

Khojimatov, Olim K. "Some Aspects of Morphology, Conservation of Resource Potential, Crop Cultivation and Harvesting of Raw Materials of Promising *Ferula* Species." *Ethnobotany Research & Applications* 22 (2021) 1–8.

Kierkegaard, Søren. "'Look at the Birds of the Air; Look at the Lily in the Field'" In *Without Authority*, edited and translated by Howard V. Hong and Edna H. Hong, 7–20. Princeton: Princeton University Press, 1997.

Kiers, Annemieke M. "Endive, Chicory, and Their Wild Relatives. A Systematic and Phylogenetic Study of *Cichorium* (*Asteraceae*)." *Gorteria. Supplement* 5.1 (2000) 1–77.

Kockmann, Norbert. "History of Distillation." In *Distillation Fundamentals and Principles*, edited by Andrzej Górak and Eva Sorensen, 1–43. Amsterdam: Elsevier, 2014.

Kim, Sung Mee, and Kwang Lee. "A Study on the Agricultural Products Mentioned in the Bible with Priority to the Cereals." *Journal of the East Asian Dietary Life* 8.4 (1998) 441–53. In Korean with English abstract.

———. "A Study of Fruits Mentioned in the Bible." *Journal of the East Asian Dietary Life* 9.2 (1999) 149–60. In Korean with English abstract.

Kislev, Mordechai E., et al. "Flax Seed Production: Evidence from the Early Iron Age Site of Tel Beth-Shean, Israel and from Written Sources." *Vegetation History and Archaeobotany* 20 (2011) 579–84.

Koh, Andrew J., et al. "Phoenician Cedar Oil from Amphoriskoi at Tel Kedesh: Implications Concerning Its Production, Use and Export during the Hellenistic Age." *Bulletin of the American Schools of Oriental Research* 385 (2021) 99–117.

Koops, Robert G. *Each According to Its Kind: Plants and Trees of the Bible. Helps for Translators*. Reading, UK: United Bible Society, 2012.

———. "Flora in Ezra, Nehemiah, and Esther." *The Bible Translator* 51.2 (2000) 232–39.

Köbbing, Jan Felix, et al. "The Utilisation of Reed (*Phragmites australis*): A Review." *Mires and Peat* 13 (2013/14) 1–14 (Article 01)

Langgut, Dafna. "Prestigious Fruit Trees in Ancient Israel: First Palynological Evidence for Growing *Juglans regia* and *Citrus medica*." *Israel Journal of Plant Sciences* 62.1–2 (2015) 98–110.

Langgut, Dafna, and Kathryn Gleason. "Identification of the Miniaturised Garden of King Herod the Great: The Fossil Pollen Evidence." *Strata: Bulletin of the Anglo-Israel Archaeological Society* 38 (2020) 73–101.

Lemmelijn, Bénédicte. "Flora in Cantico Canticorum: Towards a More Precise Characterisation of Translation Technique in the LXX of Song of Songs." *Supplements to the Journal for the Study of Judaism* 126 (2008) 27–52.

Liber et al. "The History of Lentil (*Lens culinaris* subsp. *culinaris*) Domestication and Spread as Revealed by Genotyping-by-Sequencing of Wild and Landrace Accessions." *Frontiers in Plant Science* 12 (2021) 1–18 (article 628439).

Léon-Gonzáles, Antonio J., et al. "Genus *Retama*: A Review on Traditional Uses, Phytochemistry, and Pharmacological Activities." *Phytochemistry Reviews* 17 (2018) 701–31.

Levey, Martin. "The Early History of Detergent Substances: A Chapter in Babylonian Chemistry." *Journal of Chemical Education* 31.10 (1954) 521–24.

Liphschitz, Nili. "*Ceratonia siliqua* in Israel: An Ancient Element or a Newcomer." *Israel Journal of Botany* 36.4 (1987) 191–97.

Liphschitz, Nili, and Gideon Biger. "Past Distribution of Aleppo Pine *(Pinus halepensis)* in the Mountains of Israel (Palestine)." *The Holocene* 11.4 (2001) 427–36.

Liphschitz, Nili, et al. "Dendroarchaeological Investigations in Israel (Masada)." *Israel Exploration Society* 31 (1981) 230–34.

Liss, Brady, et al. "Up the Wadi: Development of an Iron Age Industrial Landscape in Faynan, Jordan." *Journal of Field Archeology* 45.6 (2020) 413–27. DOI: 10.1080/00934690.2020.1747792.

Littman, Robert J., et al. "Eau de Cleopatra Mendesian Perfume and Tell Timai." *Near Eastern Archaeology* 84.3 (2021) 216–21.

López-Sampson, Arlene, and Tony Page. "History and Use and Trade of Agarwood." *Economic Botany* 72.1 (2018) 107–29.

Lucas, A. "Notes on Myrrh and Stacte." *The Journal of Egyptian Archaeology* 23.1 (1937) 27–33.

Luzzatto, Lucio, and Paolo Arese. "Favism and Glucose-6-Phosphate Dehydrogenase Deficiency." *New England Journal of Medicine* 378 (2018) 60–71.

Mabberley, David J., and Henry J. Noltie. "A Note on *Valeriana jatamansi* Jones (Caprifoliaceae s.l.)." *Blumea* 59 (2014) 37–41.

Maeder, Felicitas. "Byssus and Sea Silk: A Linguistic Problem with Consequences." In *Treasures from the Sea: Sea Silk and Shellfish Purple Dye in Antiquity*, edited by Hedvig Enegren and Francesco Meo, 4–19. Oxford: Oxbow, 2017.

McDonald, J. Andrew. "Influences of Egyptian Lotus Symbolism and Ritualistic Practices on Sacral Tree Worship in the Fertile Crescent from 1500 BCE to 200 CE." *Religions* 9.9 (2018) 256. DOI:10.3390/rel9090256.

Meiggs, Russell. *Trees and Timber in the Ancient Mediterranean World*. Oxford: Oxford University Press, 1982.

Merlin, M. D. "Archaeological Evidence for the Tradition of Psychoactive Plant Use in the Old World." *Economic Botany* 57 (2003) 295–323.

Meshorer, Ya'akov. *Ancient Jewish Coinage. Volume 1: Persian Period through Hasmonaeans*. Dix Hills, NY: Amphora, 1962.

Milia, Egle, et al. "Leaves and Fruits Preparations of *Pistacia lentiscus* L.: A Review on the Ethnopharmalogical Uses and Implications in Inflammation and Infection." *Antibiotics* 10.4 (2021) 425. DOI:10.3390/antibiotics10040425

Miller, James Innes. *The Spice Trade of the Roman Empire, 29 B.C. to A.D.* Oxford: Clarendon, 1969.

Miller-Naudé, Cynthia A., and Jacobus A. Naudé. "Alerity in Bible Translation." In *A Guide to Bible Translation: People, Languages, and Topics*, edited by Philip A. Noss and Charles S. Houser, 290–94. Swindon, UK: United Bible Societies, 2019.

Mills, J. S., and R. White. "The Identity of the Resins from the Late Bronze Shipwreck at Ulu Burun." *Archaeometry* 31.1 (1989) 37–44.

Molari, Luisas, et al. "*Arundo donax*: A Widespread Plant with Great Potential as Sustainable Structural Material." *Construction and Building Materials* 268 (2021) 121143. https://doi.org/10.1016/j.conbuildmat.2020.121143. [Cane building]

Moldenke, Harold N., and Alma L. Moldenke. *Plants of the Bible.*[2] New York: Ronald Press, 1952.

---

2. There are numerous reprints.

Moore, George F. "The Caper-Plant and Its Edible Products. With Reference to Eccles. XII.5." *Journal of Biblical Literature* 10.1 (1891) 55–64.

Moorey, P. Roger S. *Ancient Mesopotamian Materials and Industries.* Reprint, Winona Lake, IN: Eisenbrauns, 1994.

Mukkaddasi. *Description of Syria Including Palestine.* Translated and annotated by Guy Le Strange. 1886. Reprint, London: Forgotten, 2008.

Murray, Mary Anne. "Cereal Production and Processing." In *Ancient Egyptian Materials and Technology*, edited by Paul T. Nicholson and Ian Shaw, 520–26. Cambridge: University Press, 2000.

———. "Fruits, Vegetables, Pulses, and Condiments." In *Ancient Egyptian Materials and Technology*, edited by Paul T. Nicholson and Ian Shaw, 268–98. Cambridge: Cambridge University Press, 2000.

Musselman, Lytton John. "The Botanical Activities of George Edward Post (1838–1909)." *Archives of Natural History* 33.2 (2006) 282–31.

———. *A Dictionary of Bible Plants.* Cambridge: University Press, 2011.

———. *Figs, Dates, Laurel, and Myrrh: Plants of the Bible and the Qur'an.* Portland, OR: Timber, 2007.

———. "Solomon's Plant Life: Plant Lore and Image in the Solomonic Writings." *Perspectives on Science and Christian Faith* 51.10 (1999) 1–8.

Musselman, Lytton John, and Peter W. Schafran. *Edible Wild Plants of the Carolinas.* Chapel Hill, NC: University of North Carolina Press, 2021.

Nair, Kodoth Prabhakaran. "Asafoetida or Asafetida." In *Minor Spices and Condiments Global Economic Potential,* 185–91. New York: Springer, 2021.

Naudé, Jacobus A., and Cynthia L. Miller-Naudé. "Lexicography and the Translation of 'Cedars of Lebanon' in the Septuagint." *HTS Teologiese Studies/Theological Studies* 74.3 (2018) 1–3.

Naudé, Jacobus A., and Cynthia L. Miller-Naudé. "Sacred Writings and Their Translations as Complex Phenomena: The Book of Ben Sira in the Septuagint as a Case in Point." In *Complexity Thinking in Translation Studies. Methodological Considerations*, edited by Kobus Marais & Reine Meylaerts, 180–215. London: Routledge, 2019.

Nazar, Sonaima, et al. "*Capparis decidua* Edgew. (Forssk.)[sic]: A Comprehensive Review of Its Traditional Uses, Phytochemistry, Pharmacology and Nutrapharmaceutical." *Arabian Journal of Chemistry* 13 (2020) 1901–16.

Nemu, Danny. "Getting High with the Most High: Entheogens in the Old Testament." *Journal of Psychedelic Studies* 3.2 (2019) 117–32.

Oomah, B. Dave. "Flaxseed as a Functional Food Source." *Journal of the Sciences of Food and Agriculture* 81.9 (2001) 889–94.

Orendi, Andrea. "Flax Cultivation in the Southern Levant and Its Development during the Bronze and Iron Age." *Quaternary International* 545 (2020) 63–72.

Paris, Harry S. "Origin and Emergence of the Sweet Dessert Watermelon, *Citrullus lanatus*." *Annals of Botany* 116.2 (2015) 133–48.

Pendergast, Hew D. V. "Pollen Cakes of *Typha* spp. [Typhaceae]—'Lost' and Living Food." *Economic Botany* 54.3 (2000) 254–55.

Poole, J. P., and Ronald Reed. "The Preparation of Leather and Parchment by the Dead Sea Scrolls Community." *Technology and Culture* 3.1 (1962) 1–26.

Porwal, Omji, et al. "*Silybum marianum* (Milk Thistle): Review on Its Chemistry, Morphology, Ethno Medical Uses, Phytochemistry and Pharmacological Activities." *Journal of Drug Delivery and Therapeutics* 9.5 (2019) 199–206.

Prado, Shalen. "Esoteric Botanical Knowledge-scapes of Medieval Iberia." *Archaeological Review from Cambridge* 35.2 (2020) 98–111.

Puhlman, Marie-Luise, and Willem M. de Vos. "Back to the Roots: Revisiting the Use of the Fiber-Rich *Cichorium intybus* L. Taproots." *Advances in Nutrition* 11 (2020) 878–89.

Pullaiah, T., and B. N. Divakara. "Wood Uses, Ethnobotany and Pharmacognosy." In *Red Sanders: Silviculture and Conservation*, edited by T. Pullaiah et al., 17–34. Singapore: Springer, 2019.

Quillien, Louise. "Dissemination and Price of Cotton in Mesopotamia during the 1st Millennium BCE." *Revue d'Ethnoécologie* (2019). https://doi.org/10.4000/ethnoecologie.4239.

Ramadan, Mohamed Fawzy. *Black Cumin* (Nigella sativa) *Seeds: Chemistry, Technology, Functionality, Applications*. Cham, Switzerland: Springer, 2021.

Renaut, Luc. "Recherches sur le Henné Antique." *Journal of Near Eastern Studies*. 68.3 (2009) 19–212.

Rackham, Harris, trans. *Pliny Natural History Books XII–XVI*. Loeb Classical Library. IV(XIII). 1945. Reprint, Cambridge: Harvard University Press, 1986.

Rousou, Maria, et al. "Identification of Archaeobotanical *Pistacia* L. Fruit Remains: Implications for Our Knowledge on Past Distribution and Use in Prehistoric Cyprus." *Vegetation History and Archaeobotany* 30 (2021) 623–39.

Royle, John F. "Baca." In *Cyclopedia of Biblical Literature*, Volume 1, edited by John Kitto, 276–77. New York: American Book Exchange, 1880

———. "Lily." In *Cyclopedia of Biblical Literature*, Volume 2, edited by John Kitto, 250–51. New York: American Book Exchange, 1880.

Salehi, Bahare, et al. "Nigella Plants—Traditional Uses, Bioactive phytoconstituents, Preclinical and Clinical Studies." *Frontiers in Pharmacology* 12 (2021) article 625386.

Sallon, Sarah al. "Origins and Insights into the Historic Judean Date Palm Based on Genetic Analysis of Germinated Ancient Seeds and Morphometric Studies." *Science Advances* 6.6 (2020) DOI:10.1126/sciadv.aax0384.

Samuel, Delwen. "Bread Making and Social Interactions at the Amarna Workmen's Village, Egypt." *World Archaeology* 31.1 (1999) 121–44.

———. "Brewing and Baking." In *Ancient Egyptian Materials and Technology*, edited by Paul T. Nicholson and Ian Shaw, 537–76. Cambridge: Cambridge University Press, 2000.

Sarpaki, Anaya. "The Archaeology of Garlic (*Allium sativum*): The Find at Akrotiri, Thera, Greece." *Documenta Praehistorica XLVIII* (2021) 2–15.

Schearing, Linda S., and Valarie H. Ziegler. *Enticed by Eden: How Western Culture Uses, Confuses (and Sometimes Abuses) Adam and Eve*. Waco, TX: Baylor University Press, 2013.

Scott, Ashley, et al. "Exotic Foods Reveal Contact between South Asia and the Near East during the Second Millennium BCE." *Proceedings of the National Academy of Sciences* 118.2 (2021) e2014956117.

Seignobos, Christian, and Jacques Schwendiman. "Traditional Cotton Plants in Cameroon." *Cotton and Tropical Fibres* 46.4 (1991) 322–33.

Shemesh, Abraham Ofir. "'The Rabbis Maintained That It Was Flaxseed': The Identification and Interpretation of Unidentified Biblical Plants in Aggadic Homilies." *Biblical Theology Bulletin* 49.3 (2019) 156–68.
Singh, K. B., and Mohan C. Saxena. *Chickpeas*. New York: Macmillan, 1999.
van Sladen, Michiel, and Thomas Payne. "Concepts and Nomenclature of the Farro Wheats, with Special Reference to Emmer." *Kew Bulletin* 68.3 (2013) 477–94.
Spiers, William Quiver. "Flower Teachings: The Perils of Greatness." *The Quiver: An Illustrated Magazine of Social, Intellectual, and Religious Progress* 22 (1887) 637–41.
Steiner, Richard C. *Stockmen from Tekoa, Sycomores from Sheba: A Study of Amos' Occupations*. Catholic Biblical Quarterly Monograph Series 36. Washington, DC, Catholic Biblical Association, 2003.
Steinmann, Andrew E. "He Is Like a Tree: Arboreal Imagery for Humans in Biblical Wisdom Literature." *Religions* 12.10 (2021) 804.
Suderman, W. Derek. "Modest or Magnificent? Lotus Versus Lily in Canticles." *The Catholic Biblical Quarterly* 67.1 (2005) 42–58.
Thulin, Mats. "The Genus *Boswellia* (Burseraceae) The Frankincense Trees." *Symbolae Botanicae Upsaliensis* 39 (2020) 52–61.
Trakoli, Anna. "Minoan Art, The 'Saffron Gatherers', c1650 BC." *Occupational Medicine* 71 (2021) 124–26.
Trever, John C. "The Flora of the Bible and Biblical Scholarship." *Journal of Bible and Religion* 27.1 (1959) 45–49.
van der Veen, Marijke. "The Economic Value of Chaff and Straw in Arid and Temperate Zones." *Vegetation History and Archaeobotany* 8 (1999) 211–24.
Villar, Jose L., et al. "Out of the Middle East: New Phylogenetic Insights in the Genus *Tamarix* (Tamaricaceae)." *Journal of Systematics and Evolution* 57.5 (2018) 488–507.
de Vries, I. M. "Origin and Domestication of *Lactuca sativa* L." *Genetic Resources and Crop Evolution* 44 (1997) 165–74.
Vogelsang-Eastwood, Gillian. "Textiles." In *Ancient Egyptian Materials and Technology*, edited by Paul T. Nicholson and Ian Shaw, 268–98. Cambridge: Cambridge University Press, 2000.
Walker, David J., et al. "*Atriplex halimus* L.: Its Biology and Uses." *Journal of Arab Environments* 100–101 (2014) 411–21.
Walter, Tilmann, et al. "The Emperor's Herbarium: The German Physician Leonhard Rauwolf (1535–96) and his Botanical Field Studies in the Middle East." *History of Science*. https://doi.org/10.1177/00732753211019848.
Waniakowa, Jadwiga. "Mandragora and Belladonnna—the Names of Two Magic Plants." *Studia Linguistica Universitatus Iagellonicae Cracoviensis* 124 (2007) 161–73.
Wasylikowa, Krystnyna, and Marijke van der Veen. "An Archaeobotanical Contribution to the History of Watermelon, *Citrullus lanatus* (Thunb.) Matsum. & Nakai (syn. *C. vulgaris* Schrad.)." *Vegetation History and Archaeobotany* 13 (2004) 213–17.
Wendrich, Willemina Z. "Basketry." In *Ancient Egyptian Materials and Technology*, edited by Paul T. Nicholson and Ian Shaw, 254–67. Cambridge: Cambridge University Press, 2000.
Whitlam, Jade et al. "Cutting the Mustard: New Insights into the Plant Economy of Late Neolithic Tepe Khaleseh (Iran)." *Iran Journal of the British Institute of Persian Studies* 58.2 (2020) 149–66.

Zaccai, Michele, et al. "*Lilium candidum*: Flowering Characterization of Wild Israeli Ecotypes." *Israel Journal of Plant Sciences* 57.4 (2009) 297–302.

Zorgati, Ragnhild Johnsrud. "The Green Line of the Jerusalem Code: Trees, Flowers, Science, and Politics." In *Tracing the Jerusalem Code*, Volume 3, edited by R. J. Zorgati et al., 329–59. Berlin: De Gruyter, 2021.

Zohary, Michael. *Plants of the Bible*. Cambridge: Cambridge University Press, 1982.

Zohary, Daniel, et al. *Domestication of Plants in the Old World: The Origin and Spread of Domesticated Plants in South-West Asia, Europe, and the Mediterranean Basin*. Oxford: Oxford University Press, 2012.

Bible Translations

ASV	Authorized Standard Version
ESV	English Standard Version
Darby or JND	Authorized Version of John Nelson Darby
DRA	Douay-Rheims Version
Geneva Bible	
KJV (or AV)	King James Version (formally: the Authorized Version)
MSG	The Message
NASB	New American Standard Bible
NIV	New International Version
NJB	New Jerusalem Bible
NKJV	New King James Version
NLT	New Living Translation
RSV	Revised Standard Version

Subject Index

Abies cilicica. See Cilician fir
Abraham, 258, 259
Absalom, 236, 267
Absinthe, 302
Acacia, 3–6, 267
Acacia albida, 6
Acacia tortilis, 4
Acer pseudoplatanus, 255
Acorns. See oak
Acorus calamus, 47
Acorus gramineus, 47
Adwa, Ethiopia, 118
Aleppo pine, 209, 224–25, 228
Alexandria, Egypt, 173
Algeria, 279
Algum, 8, 13
Allium cepa. See onion
Allium kurrat. See leek
Allium porrum. See leek
Allium sativum. See garlic
Almond, 10–13
Almug, 8, 12, 14
Aloe, xxi, 71, 196, 249
Aloeswood, xxi, 17–18
Aloe vera, xxi, 17
Amman, Jordan, 40, 46, 188, 242, 252
Amorite, 293
Anemone, 119, 148, 179, 189, 181, 182
Anemone coronaria, 119, 179
Anointing oil, 51, 71, 211
Antakya, Turkey, 217, 277, 131
Anthemum graveolens, 102
Antioch. See Antakya
Aphrodisiac, 56, 156

Apple, xxi, 21–23
Apricot, 10, 22–23
Aquilaria malaccensis, 19
Araar. See thyine
Arabian Peninsula, 13, 124, 258
Arabic, 91, 98, 156, 172, 191, 229, 271, 279, 281, 292
Aramaic, xiv
Artemisia herba-alba, 302
Arugula, 136, 192
Arundo donax, 51
Asafoetida, 127, 129
Assyria, 66, 181, 225
Astralagus, 151
Astragalus tragacanthus, 267
Atlas Mountains, ix, 241, 279
Atriplex halimus. See mallow,
Ayurvedic medicine, 47, 50, 252
Azraq Oasis, 242

Babylon, 14, 67, 71, 110, 237, 224, 278
Balaam, 17, 18, 97
Balm, 163–64, 197
Balm of Gilead, 163–64, 196, 197, 267
Barley, xviii, 8, 24–26, 30
  Beer, 26, 29
  Chaff, 291
  Gluten, 26–27
  Harvest, 27–28
  Hulled, 26
  Pearled, 26
  Threshing floor, 175–76
Bashan, 208
Baskets, 52, 220, 225, 289, 292, 299

318 SUBJECT INDEX

Bay leaves, 169
Bean, 30–31, 218, 292
    Broad, 31, 172
    Garbanzo, 31–34, 104
Beer, 26–27, 30, 289, 293
Beersheba, 44
Beirut, ix, xi
Bethlehem, 25–26, 176, 217
Bible translations, xix
Bitter herbs, 35
Bitumen, 225
Black cumin, 37–40
Boaz, 26
Boswellia species, 124
Boswellia neglecta, 125, 126
Boswellia sacra, 126
Boxwood, 8–9
Brassicaceae, 192
Brassica alba. See *Sinapis alba*
Brassica nigra, 192
Bread, xxi, 24–26, 29, 30, 35, 38, 91, 156, 140, 164, 208, 212, 268, 289, 292
Bread wheat. See wheat
Bricks, 291, 295
Broadbean. See beans.
Broom, 44–46
Bulrush. See papyrus
Buxus sempervirens, 8
Byblos, Lebanon, 57

Calabrian pine. See *Pinus brutia*
Calamus, 47, 51
Calypso, 278
Cane
    Fragrant. See calamus
    Giant. See *Arundo donax*
Caper, xix, 56–59
Capparis spinosa. See caper
Caraway, 91
Carob, 61–62
Carrot, 130
Cashew, 229
Cassia, 71
Cattail, 63–65
Cedar of Lebanon, 66–70
Cedrus libani. See cedar of Lebanon
Centaurea solstitialis, 276

Cephalaria syriaca, 262
Ceratonia siliqua. See carob
Chaff, 290–91, 295
Charcoal, xvi, 44, 175, 208
Chate melon. See melon
Chickpea, 31–32
Chicory, 35
Chouf Cedar Preserve, Mount Lebanon 36
Cicer arietinum. See chickpea
Cichorium intybus. See chicory
Cilantro, 76
Cilician fir, 93, 224
Cinnamomum cassia, 71
Cinnamomum tamala, 74
Cinnamomum verum, 71
Cinnamon, 71–75
Cistus creticus, 163
Cistus salvifolius, 163
Citron wood. See thyine
Citrullus colocynthis. See gourd
Citrullus lanatus. See melon
Coffin, 255
Colycinth. See gourd
Coniine, 130
Conium maculatum, 130–34
Coriander, 76–79
Coriandrum sativum. See coriander
Cotton, 80–82, 116
Crocus sativus, 249–51
Crown of thorns and thornbush, 83–87
Cucumber, 88–90
Cucumis melo sub. *melo*. See cucumber
Cucumis sativus. See cucumber
Cumin (cummin), 91–92
    black, 38–40
Cuminum cyminum. See cumin
Cupressus sempervirens. See cypress
Cyperus papyrus. See papyrus
Cypress, 67, 93–96, 160, 224, 225
Cyprus, 67, 122, 129, 232

Dalbergia melanoxylon, 107
Damascus, 13, 52, 54, 112, 123, 159, 292
Daniel, xvii
Darnel. See tares
Date palm, 97–101

SUBJECT INDEX 319

Fruits, 100
Wood, 100
David, xiii, 31, 155, 211, 236, 259, 267
Dead Sea, 258, 259
Dill, 38, 102–3
Diospyros ebenum. See ebony
Dove's dung, 106

Easter lily. See *Lilium candidum*
Ebony, 107–9
Echinops minima, 274
Egypt, xx, xxi, 4, 8, 26, 31, 35, 38, 88,
    91, 102, 135, 149, 155, 163,
    164, 172–73, 179, 180, 187,
    218, 220, 243, 255, 256, 262,
    267, 286, 289
Elijah, 44
Elisha, 24, 138, 192
Eruca sativa. See arugula
Euphrates River, 237, 239, 242, 244
Ezekiel's bread, xxii

Faidherbia albida. See *Acacia alba*
Feast of Tabernacles, 202, 203
Ferula assa-foetida, 129
Ficus carica. See fig
Ficus sycomorus. See sycomore fig
Fig, 110–14
    Cursed, 110
    Flower, 111, 113
    Pollination, 111
    Poultice, xxi, 10,
    Sycamore fig. See sycomore fig
    Wasp, 113
Fir. See Cicilian fir
Fitches, 38
Flax, 115–18
Flour, 25, 28, 290
Flower of the field, 119–24
Fodder, 26, 60, 146, 256, 262, 289, 290,
    292, 303
Frankincense, 124–26, 127, 196, 197,
    200, 201, 249, 253
Fuel grass, 244, 262, 291, 293
Fuel wood, 4, 45

Galbanum, 127–29

Galilee, 143, 145, 158, 171, 208, 215,
    235, 269
Gall, xx, 130–34, 302
Gall, insect, 111, 207–8, 210
Garbanzo bean. See chickpea
Garlic, 135–37
Geranium libanoticum, 68
Gilead, 163
Gladiolus, 189
Gluten, 289
Gum, 149–50
Gourd, xxi, 138–39
Grain,, green, roasted. See wheat
Grape, xiv, 26, 83, 112, 140–45, 184
    Flowers, 140
    Green, 141
    Juice, 141
    Leaves, 141
    Pruning, 145
    Sour, 141–42
    Sour grape power, 142
    Wood, 142
Gundelia tournefortii. See tumbleweed

Hapex legemenon, xviii, 135
Hauran, 208
Hebron, 147, 194, 29
Hemlock, poison. See gall
Henna, xviii, 151–54
Hula Swamp, 220
Hyssop, 155–60

Incense, 14, 17, 124, 127, 149, 196,
    197, 198, 252, 267
Ink, 208
International Center for Agricultural
    Research in the Dry Areas 33,
    35, 77, 186, 296

Jacob, 149, 163, 176, 229, 231, 237, 267
Jeremiah, 110, 130
Jericho, 97, 256
Jerusalem, 83, 86, 98, 249, 251
Jesus, 18, 25, 51, 98, 110–11, 130–31,
    140, 180–81, 191–93, 252, 256,
    262–63
Jezebel, 44
John the Baptist, 281

SUBJECT INDEX

Jordan River, 63, 245
Jordan Valley, 63, 119, 192, 237
Joseph, 149, 164
Jotham, xiii-xiv, 83
Juglans regia. See walnut
Juniper, 44, 67, 160-62
Juniperus drupacea. See juniper
Juniperus excelsa. See juniper
Juniperus oxycedrus. See juniper
Juniperus phoenicea. See juniper

King Hezekiah, xxi, 111-12
King Hiram, 8, 66, 93
King Saul, 166, 259
King Solomon. See Solomon
King of Tyre, 8, 66, 93
Kufur Sumei, Israel, 143, 171, 215

Lactuca serriola. See bitter herbs
Ladanum, 163-65
Lampstand, 11, 211
Latakia, Syria, 27, 265
Laurel, 169-71
Laurus nobilis. See laurel
Lawsonia inermis. See henna
Leather preservative, 208, 211
Leaven, 193
Leek, 172-74
Legumes, 31, 63, 175
Lens culinaris. See lentil
Lentil, 30, 175-78, 218
Leprosy, 67
Lettuce. See bitter herbs
Lign aloes, 17
Lilium candidum, 179
Lily of the field, 179-80
Lily of the valley, 180
Linen, 80-81
Linum usitatissimum. See flax
Locust bean gum. See carob
Lolium temulentum. See tares
Lotus, 63

Mallow, 185-86
Malta, 279
Malus pumila. See apple
Mandragora officinarum. See mandrake

Mandrake, 187-88, 293
Manna, xx, xxii, 76-79
Mary of Bethany, 252
Masada, 258
Measuring
    Line, 115
    Reed, 51
    Rod, 51
Medaba, Jordan, 288, 293
Melon
    Chate melon. See cucumber
    Watermelon, 138, 286-88
Menorah. See lampstand
Mentha arvensis, 190
Mentha longifolia, 189
Mesopotamia, 18, 218, 293
Millet, xxii, 146
Mint, 189-90
Moses, 135, 220, 225, 289
Mount Lebanon 8, 12, 66, 67, 147, 160, 170, 226, 227, 233, 268
Mount Tabor, 208, 270
Mulberry, xxi, 236, 255, 266,
Mustard, xxi, 35, 191-95, 255
    Black, 192, 195
    White, 192, 195
Myrrh, xxi, 151, 163, 196-201, 249, 253
Myrtle, 47, 202-5
Myrtus communis. See myrtle

Narcissus, 180, 183
Narcissus tazetta. See narcissus
Narcotic, xx
Nard. See spikenard
Nardostachys jatamansi. See spikenard
Nettle, 205-307
Nigella sativa. See black cumin
Nightshade, 187
Nile River, 220
    Delta, 155, 220
    Valley, 31
Noah's ark, 3, 225
Nut tree. See walnut
Nymphea caerulea, 179
Nymphaea nouchali, 180

Oak, 207-11
    Acorns, 207, 208, 211

Aleppo oak, 209
Bashan, 208
Hauran, 208
Kermes oak, 209
Wood, 208
Valonia oak, 209
Oak-pine forest type, 197
Oak-terebinth forest type, 266
Odyssey, 278
Ointment, 211, 252
Olea europea. See olive
Olive, xxi, xiii, 83, 110, 175
    Condiment, 76
    Flower, 213, 217
    Leaves, 212
    Oil, 156, 211–12, 281
    Sprouts, 212
    Wild, 213
    Wood, 212
Onion, 30, 135, 172, 218–19, 28
Onopordum acanthium, 273
Ophir, 13
Opium poppy, xx-xxi, 121, 122, 130, 131
Oregano, 155
Origanum syriacum. See hyssop
Ox, 290, 294

Palm. See date palm
Palmyra, Syria, 97, 303
Papaver rhoeas. See flower of the field
Papaver somniferum. See gall
Paper, 220
Papyrus, 220–24
Passover, 35
Paul the Apostle, 169
Pennisetum americanum. See millet
Perfume, 14
Perfumed wood. See thyine
Phoenix dactylifera. See date palm
Phragmites australis. See reed
Pillar, 178–79, 234
Pine 93, 149, 163, 164, 196, 224–28
    Aleppo pine, 209, 224–25, 228
    Calabrian pine, 224, 225, 227
    Resin, 225
    Stone pine, 224
    Umbrella. See stone pine

Pinus brutia. See Calabrian pine
Pinus halepensis. See Aleppo pine
Pinus pinea. See stone pine
Pistacia. See terebinth
Pistachio, 229–31
Pistacia atlantica. See terebinth
Pistacia lentiscus. See terebinth
Pistacia lentiscus var. *chio.* See terebinth
Pistacia lentiscus var. *lentiscus.* See terebinth
Pitch, 225
Plane tree, 231–34, 236
Platanus occidentalis. See plane tree
Platanus orientalis. See plane tree
Pliny, 278
Poa bulbosa, 147
Poison hemlock. See gall
Pomegranate, 234–35
Poplar, 236–42
    Euphrates, 236–40
    White, 237, 241
Poppy. See flower of the field
Populus alba. See white poplar
Populus euphratica. See Euphrates poplar
Populus tremuloides, 237
Post, George Edward, xvi
Prunus armeniaca. See almond
Prunus dulcis. See almond
Pterocarpus santalinus. See red sanders
Punica granatum. See pomegranate
Pyrus malus. See apple

Queen of Sheba, 13
Quercus calliprinos, 207
Quercus coccifera. See *Quercus calliprinos*
Quercus infectoria, 209
Quercus ithaburensis, 207
Quercus infectoria, 209
Quill, 243

Radicchio, 3
Rahab, 115
Raisin, 141, 292
Ramallah, Palestinian Territories, 219
Red heifer offering, 67, 155

Red sanders, 3, 15–16
Reed, 51, 242–46
Retama raetam. See broom
Retting, 115
Reuben, 118, 293
Rose of Sharon, xx, xxi, 178
Rue, 91, 247–48
Ruta chalepensis. See rue
Ruta graveolens. See rue

Saffron, 249–51
Sahara, 286
Sahel, 3
Salix acmophylla, 301
Salix alba, 301
Salix babylonica, 299
Salix caprea, 300
Saltbush. See mallow
Salt herbs, 185
Salvadora persica, 191
Sandalwood, 8, 13, 14, 16, 212
Sandarac, 279, 289
Santalum album. See sandalwood
Sarcopoterium spinosum, 83
Segetal, 180, 262, 263
Serotinous cone, 225
Shechem, 149
Silybum marianum, 277
Silk, 81
Sinai, 3, 155
Sinapis arvense, 192
Soap, 211, 213, 225
Socrates, 130
Solomon, xiii–xiv, 66, 93, 97, 138, 98, 156, 179, 180, 196
Spikenard, 252–54
Spiny burnet, 83, 86–87
Star of Bethlehem, 104–6
Straw, 292–93, 295
Storax, xix, 197
Styrax, 197
Suweida, Syria, 90
Sweet cane. See calamus
Sweet myrtle, 47
Sycamine. See sycomore fig
Sycamore. See sycomore fig
Sycomore fig, 255–58
Syconium, 111, 255

Syrian hyssop, 155
Tabernacle, 3, 11
Tamarisk, 258–61
Tamarix aphylla, 258
Tamarix gallica, 260
Tamarix nilotica, 258
Tannin, 207, 208, 235
Tares, 191, 262–66
Temper, brick, 289, 291
Terebinth 163, 197, 207, 225, 229, 259, 266–70
Testes, 56
Tetraclinis articulata. See thyine
Theophrastus, 278
Thistle, xix, 264, 271–77, 281
Threshing, 290
    Floor, 26, 175, 176
    Sledge, 26
Thyine, 253, 278–80
Tigris River, 237, 238, 242, 301,
Tubas, Palestinian Territories, 40, 116
Tulip, 179, 180
Tumbleweed, 281–83
Typha laxmannii. See cattail
Tyre, 257

Vicia faba. See broadbean
Vinegar, 51, 141, 196
Vitis vinifera. See grape

Wadi Arabah, Jordan, 45, 84, 85
Wadi Jhanem, Lebanon, 136
Walnut, xiii, 284–85
Watermelon, 138, 286–88
Wetland, 51, 63, 181, 185, 242
Wheat, xviii, 24, 25, 115, 146, 187, 262, 264, 282, 289–98
    Bread, 289
    Chaff, 290, 291
    Durum, 289, 290
    Emmer, 289
    Free-threshing, 290
    Germ, 290
    Green, roasted, 291–92
    Hulled, 290
    Straw, 292–93
    Threshing, 290, 294
    Weeds, 293

Winnowing, 290, 291
Wick, 115
Wilderness of Judea, 25
Wild greens, 185
Willow, 299–301
Wine, 141
Wine amphora, 141, 225

Winnowing, 27, 28, 290, 291
With (withe). See willow
Wormwood, 302–3

za'atar, 156
Zacchaeus, 256
Ziziphus spina-christi, 83

Scripture Index
(in alphabetic order)

Acts
10:6	214

Amos
2:9	214
7:14	

1 Chronicles
10:12	268, 276
14:14	244, 275
16:17	275
27:28	219

2 Chronicles
1:15	264
2:8	9
3:16	242
9:27	264
28:15	101

Daniel
1:12	32
4:22	xvii

Deuteronomy
8:7–9	26, 102, 299
23:24	24, 146
25:4	28
24:6	300
28:40	219
32:13	220
34:3	101

Esther
8:15	85

Exodus
9:31–32	27, 300
12:8	38
12:22	161
15:27	101
16:31	80
20:23	50
25:33–34	13, 242
30:4	272
30:23–24	75, 291
30:34–35	132
37:38	3

Ezekiel
4:9	xxii, 181
15:2	2, 147
18:2	146
27:5	5, 97
27:15	115
27:17	170
27:19	75
31:2–3	70
31:8	228
40:3	54
41:18	102
42:16–18	54

Genesis

3:18	280
4:3	121
21:15	267
21:33–34	267
25:30	181
25:34	181
30:14	193, 302
30:37	239, 245
35:4	276
37:25	155, 169, 170, 232
43:11	xix, 13, 155, 169
49:22	146
51:8	170

Haggai

2:19	142

Hebrews

9:19	163

Hosea

1:13	102
4:13	276
9:6	212
10:4	135, 271
14:6	185

Isaiah

1:8	92
5:2	146
6:13	225, 276
9:14	102
14:8	71
15:7	310
17:14	292
18:2	228
18:5	145
28:25–28	41, 95
34:4	116
34:13	44
37:24	97
37:27	152
40:6	152
44:4	245, 310
44:14	276

James

1:12	175

Jeremiah

2:22	220
6:2	50
8:22	169, 170
17:8	310
22:23	70
23:15	135, 245, 313
31:29	146
51:31–32	32, 250
52:22–23	242
61:1–3	146

Job

8:11	228
15:33	147
30:3	191
30:7	212
31:40	271
40:21	67
40:22	310

Joel

1:11	102
1:12	23, 242 k

John

4:35	27
12:3–5	260
12:12–13	102, 229
19:29	146, 163
19:39	20

2 John

1:12	112

3 John

13	55

Joshua

2:1	107
5:11	302

Judges

3:13	101
4:5	102
6:11	276
6:18	143
7:13	28
9:8–15	87, 219
9:49	155

1 Kings

4:33	60, 161, 162
4:39	199
6:5	162
6:15	97
6:29	102
7:2	71
7:18	242
9:17	102
10:12	15
10:27	71, 264
19:2–4	47

2 Kings

4:38–39	143
4:42	26
6:25	109
7:1	27
9:26	152
19:23	97
20:7	116
25:17	242

Leviticus

14:37	162
23:4	102
23:14	255
23:22	28

Luke

6:21	245, 310

12:27	185
13:19	198
17:6	198
19:1	14
23:36	146

Malachi

3:2	220

Mark

4:31	195
11:20–21	115
15:19	54
15:23	203
15:36	146

Matthew

2:11	129
2:12	120
13:24–30	272
13:31	198
13:36–43	272
23:23	95, 107
27:34	135
27:48	54, 146

Nahum

2:3	98

Nehemiah

8:15	209, 221

Numbers

6:13	140, 146
11:5	92, 178, 226, 296
11:7–8	80
24:6	19, 101

1 Peter

1:24	124, 152
5:4	175

Proverbs

7:17	203
10:26	146
24:30	280
24:31	271
25:11	23
25:20	146
27:22	300

Psalms

29:5	70
45:8	19, 75
51:7	161
69:21	140
83:13	291
84:6	244
92:12–13	102
104:14–15	219
120:3–4	47
128:3	220
137:2	245

Revelation

6:6	28
11:1	54
14:20	146
18:11–12	16, 85, 288, 313
18:13	75

Romans

11:17–18	221

Ruth

2:2	28

I Samuel

12:16–17	302
17:2	276
22:6	268
31:13	268

2 Samuel

1:21	220
5:23	24, 244, 246
17:27–28	32

Song of Solomon

1:14	157
2:3	23
4:3	242
4:13–15	50, 75, 242, 260
5:5	203
5:13	181, 203
5:15	70
6:7	242
6:11	242, 294
7:7–8	23, 102
7:13	193
8:2	242
8:5	23

Zechariah

1:8–11	209

Zephaniah

2:9	212

CPSIA information can be obtained
at www.ICGtesting.com
Printed in the USA
BVHW091157160922
647219BV00015B/761